Ultimate
Turkish Cookbook

TOP 111 traditional Turkish dishes that you can cook right now

by

Slavka Bodic

Introduction

Cuisine is a style or method of cooking associated with a place of origin. Every cuisine is mainly influenced by the ingredients that are available in local markets or through trade. Bearing in mind the history of Turkey and the famous Ottoman Empire, trade and conquests, it is obvious that Turkish cuisine was influenced by other regions. However, the Empire influenced the entire Mediterranean and beyond. Religious food laws, such as Islamic dietary laws, also exercise a strong influence on this cuisine. Regional food preparation traditions, customs and ingredients often merge to create dishes unique to this part of the world. Therefore, Turkish cuisine is distinguishable because of its aromatic ingredients and simple cooking style, with less use of spices.

Turkish pastries and desserts are some of the most delicious in the world and they catch the attraction of the visitors around the year. Some of the most famous Turkish dishes you may have heard of are *halva, locums* and *Nightingale's nests, Dolma, Kefta, Kebab, Baklava* and much more. If you are planning to visit Turkey, you must try Turkish coffee too.

Turkish cuisine mainly focuses on the use of vegetables with a blend of meat (mainly beef and lamb) and light use of spices. That makes Turkish cuisine one of the most renowned and prominent cuisine all around the world.

This cookbook is all about Turkish cuisine, which ranges from salads, appetizers, pastries, soups, breakfast, main meals to desserts. In every recipe you will find a traditional taste with a balanced use of pure ingredients. Great majority of dishes are easy to make and extraordinarily tasteful.

Table of Contents

Why Turkish food?

I guess that visiting Turkey, or the once famous Ottoman Empire, sounds exotic for you. You probably know something about some great Sultans and the Turkish history. At the end of the story, Turkey is always a good choice for vacations and spending holidays. Of course, visiting Hagia Sophia and Grand Bazar in amazing Istanbul is a must, but Bodrum, Cappadocia and Ephesus should be on the list too.

Apart from lovely beaches, history and people, food is one of the key reasons to visit Turkey. I know many people who were quite surprised by how delicious the Turkish food is, and how such a vast variety of dishes exist. My Balkan friends believe that food in the entire region came from Turkey (or Ottoman Empire, to be more precise), but my Turkish friends always say: "By conquering other territories, the Ottomans always brought new spices, dishes and ingredients on table. Our food is a mixture of different influences, including the Balkan one".

I'm from the Balkan region and only a small part of Turkey (and Istanbul) belongs to this region geographically. I've been to Turkey many times and that allows me to check what needs to be adjusted in recipes that I found on the internet with local people. The same dish is prepared in different ways in different parts of Turkey, while some famous dishes that exist in Greece, Serbia or Croatia have their Turkish version.

Moreover, many people are already adjusting some well-known Turkish dishes to some needs in the modern world, such as the Mediterranean and Keto diets. I also compiled a cookbook of the recipes for the Mediterranean diet. Also, if you want to learn more about food from other Balkan countries, please check Balkan cookbook as well. Big Cookbook with 111 Greek recipes and Serbian Cookbook, with the same number of meals, is also available on Amazon.

Turkish food has spread its culinary influence throughout the world. It's renowned as some of the best cuisines in Europe! With an age-old tradition, Turkish cuisine has been greatly influenced by the East. Fish, seafood, fresh vegetables and cheese play a significant role in the dishes, mostly because of its long coastline. In contrast, meat is less popular.

Just In Case ...

Cooking Measurement Chart

Weight

imperial	metric
1/2 oz	15 g
1 oz	29 g
2 oz	57 g
3 oz	85 g
4 oz	113 g
5 oz	141 g
6 oz	170 g
8 oz	227 g
10 oz	283 g
12 oz	340 g
13 oz	369 g
14 oz	397 g
15 oz	425 g
1 lb	453 g

Measurement

cup	onces	milliliters	tbsp.
8 cup	64 oz	1895 ml	128
6 cup	48 oz	1420 ml	96
5 cup	40 oz	1180 ml	80
4 cup	32 oz	960 ml	64
2 cup	16 oz	480 ml	32
1 cup	8 oz	240 ml	16
3/4 cup	6 oz	177 ml	12
2/3 cup	5 oz	158 ml	11
1/2 cup	4 oz	118 ml	8
3/8 cup	3 oz	90 ml	6
1/3 cup	2.5 oz	79 ml	5.5
1/4 cup	2 oz	59 ml	4
1/8 cup	1 oz	30 ml	3
1/16 cup	1/2 oz	15 ml	1

Temperature

fahrenheit	celsius
100 °F	37 °C
150 °F	65 °C
200 °F	93 °C
250 °F	121 °C
300 °F	150 °C
325 °F	160 °C
350 °F	180 °C
375 °F	190 °C
400 °F	200 °C
425 °F	220 °C
450 °F	230 °C
500 °F	260 °C
525 °F	274 °C
550 °F	288 °C

SALADS

Turkish Bulgur Salad (*Kisir*)

Preparation Time: 30 minutes
Nutrition facts: 1 slice (331 Cal)

Ingredients (5 servings)

2 cups of fine bulgur
1/3 cup of extra-virgin olive oil
1/2 teaspoon of black pepper
2 cups of boiling water
1 medium onion
1 clove of garlic
1 tablespoon of sweet red pepper paste
2 medium tomatoes
2 medium cucumbers
7 green onions
A handful of parsley leaves
3 or 4 sprigs of fresh mint
1/4 cup of freshly squeezed lemon juice or pomegranate sour
1/2 teaspoon of hot red pepper flakes, to taste
Salt to taste

Preparation

Put the bulgur in a large mixing bowl. Pour the boiling water over it. The water should cover the bulgur completely, by about 1/4 inch. Add a bit more boiling water if needed. Cover the bowl with a lid or a plastic wrap, then wrap it in a towel. Set aside for about 15 minutes to allow the bulgur to soften. While the bulgur is softening, prepare your vegetables by peeling the onion and garlic and chopping them as finely as you can. Mix the chopped onion and garlic with the pepper paste and set aside.

Chop the tomatoes, cucumbers, green onions, parsley and mint in the same manner and put them in a separate bowl. Remove the cloth from the bowl of bulgur and cover. Wearing rubber gloves, fluff the bulgur up with your fingers. Drizzle lemon juice or pomegranate sour and the oil over it and toss it through with your fingers. Add the pepper paste mixture and work it evenly through the bulgur.

Add the chopped vegetables and herbs and continue tossing with your fingers until all the ingredients are evenly dispersed. Add salt and black pepper and taste for seasoning. Serve *kısır* salad right away or cover and refrigerate it for several hours. Make sure to fluff it up again with your fingers just before serving.

Bulgur and Summer Vegetable Salad

Preparation time: 30 minutes
Cooking time: 15 minutes
Nutrition facts: 1 bowl (222 Cal)

Ingredients (8 servings)

1 1/2 cups of fine bulgur

2 cups of ripe cherry tomatoes or mini heirloom tomatoes

1 bunch of fresh basil leaves

1/3 cup plus 2 tablespoons of olive oil, separately

4 cups of water

2 teaspoons of salt

1 zucchini

1 yellow summer squash

1 teaspoon of salt

Juice of 1 lemon

Preparation

In a large saucepan, add water, bulgur and salt and bring to a boil. Reduce the heat and cover the pan. Let the bulgur simmer gently until all the water evaporates. Turn off the heat and let the bulgur continue steaming and cooling down. In the meantime, prepare the vegetables. Wash and dice the squash and cut the tomatoes in halves or quarters depending on their size. Wash the basil leaves and remove stems.

In a skillet, heat 2 tablespoons of olive oil and sauté the diced squash for a few minutes, until slightly softened. Set aside and let it cool. When the bulgur is completely cool, use your fingers or a wooden spoon to separate the grains. Add the salt and toss it through. Pour in 1/3 cup of olive oil and work it through all the bulgur evenly. Add the lemon juice and mix again. Add the cooled chopped vegetables to the bulgur and toss gently but thoroughly. Add the tomatoes and basil leaves, and again, toss them through. If the basil leaves are large, you can tear them into smaller pieces before you add them. Cool to room temperature before serving.

Turkish Red Pepper and Tomato Salad

Preparation Time: 30 minutes
Cooking Time: 15 minutes
Nutrition facts: 1 bowl (222 Cal)

Ingredients (8 servings)

4 sweet red peppers

1 and 1/2 cups of walnut halves

2 large, ripe tomatoes

1 small onion

12 large garlic cloves

1 cup of Italian parsley leaves

1 tablespoon of apple cider vinegar or pomegranate concentrate

3 tablespoons of extra-virgin olive oil

1 teaspoon of hot red pepper flakes, or more to taste

1 teaspoon of salt, more to taste

1 teaspoon of sumac powder

Preparation

Wash and drain the vegetables and herbs. Cut the peppers in half and remove the stems, seeds, and white inner membranes. With a sharp dicing blade, dice the peppers as finely as you can. Peel the tomatoes, remove the watery seed portions from the inside and discard them. Dice the pulp portions in the same manner as the peppers. Do the same with the parsley leaves, onion, and garlic cloves.

Crush the walnuts into a fine powder between two sheets of wax paper, using a rolling pin. In a large, shallow dish or tray, mix all the aforementioned ingredients and spices together with your fingers. Adjust the salt to your taste. Using a fork, continue crushing the mixture little by little until it is well mashed and blended. Transfer the mashed mixture to the serving dish and garnish it with a sprinkle of sumac powder and fresh sprigs of Italian parsley.

Turkish Navy Bean Salad (*Piyaz*)

Preparation time: 20 minutes (+ overnight)
Nutrition facts: 1 bowl (383 Cal)

Ingredients (4 servings)

1 cup of dry navy beans

1 red onion

2 ripe tomatoes, sliced

1 green pepper

6 black olives

4 lemon wedges

1/3 cup of chopped parsley

1 hard-boiled egg

1/4 cup of extra virgin olive oil

4 tablespoons of vinegar

1 tablespoon of lemon juice

Salt to taste

Black pepper to taste

Hot pepper flakes

Few springs of Italian parsley

Preparation

Soak the beans in a large water bowl, cover and leave overnight. The next morning, drain the beans and put them in a pot with fresh water. Let them boil softly until tender. Allow them to cool in the water. Drain them and rinse them under cold water before you use them. Put the drained beans in a large bowl. Drizzle the vinegar on top. Cover the bowl with a lid or a plastic wrap and let it rest for about an hour.

Drain the extra vinegar from the beans. Toss the chopped vegetables and parsley with your fingers. Put the beans on a large flat serving plate or distribute them on individual salad plates. Spread the onion slices evenly over the top. In a small mixing bowl, mix the lemon juice, olive oil, salt and pepper, then drizzle it over the salad. Garnish the top with lemon wedges, black olives, slivers of hard-boiled egg and parsley sprigs.

Turkish Shepherd Salad

Preparation Time: 15 minutes
Nutrition facts: 1 bowl (197 Cal)

Ingredients (4 servings)

1 cup of chopped tomatoes
1/4 cup of chopped cucumber
2 green peppers, chopped
1 big onion, diced
1/2 bunch of parsley
2 teaspoons of sumac
Olives to garnish

Dressing
1 lemon
1/2 teaspoon of red pepper flakes
1 tablespoon of vinegar
2 tablespoons of extra-virgin olive oil
1 teaspoon of pomegranate molasses (optional)
Salt to taste

Preparation

Put the chopped vegetables in a bowl. Dice the onion in the same way, but before adding it in the bowl, massage it with sumac. Chop parsley and mix everything. To prepare the dressing, whisk together the lemon juice, vinegar, olive oil, pomegranate molasses, red pepper flakes and salt. Pour it over the salad and give it a good stir.

Cabbage Salad with Cheese and Fresh Thyme

Preparation time: 20 minutes
Nutrition facts: 1 bowl (150 Cal)

Ingredients (8 servings)

1 medium green cabbage, thinly sliced/10 cups of chopped cabbage
1 cup of sliced Pepperoncini
1 cup of crumbled white cheese (feta is good too)
1 tablespoon of fresh thyme leaves, washed and chopped
Freshly-ground black pepper to taste

Dressing

6 tablespoons of extra-virgin olive oil
3 tablespoons of red wine vinegar
1 tablespoon of fresh-squeezed lemon juice (see notes)
1 teaspoon of green seasoning
1/2 teaspoon of dried thyme/fresh thyme

Preparation

Whisk together the olive oil, red wine vinegar, lemon juice, green seasoning and either dried or fresh thyme. For dressing, measure out 1 cup of sliced Pepperoncini and 1 cup of white cheese to taste.

Wash fresh thyme in a salad spinner if needed, then pull leaves off the stems and chop coarsely to get about one tablespoon of chopped thyme leaves. Mix the desired amount of dressing into the cabbage. Stir in the fresh thyme (if using) and the sliced pepperoncini. Gently stir in the crumbled white cheese and season the salad with freshly-ground black pepper.

Turkish Classic Macaroni Salad

Preparation Time: 10 minutes
Cooking time: 10 minutes
Nutrition facts: 1 bowl (456 Cal)

Ingredients (6 servings)

1 pound of elbow macaroni
1 tablespoon of olive oil
1 cup of carrots, diced
½ cup of potatoes, diced
½ cup of frozen peas
½ cup of fresh dill, chopped
¼ cup of dill pickles, chopped
1 teaspoon of salt
1 cup of yogurt (make it thin with water)
¼ cup of mayonnaise
1 tablespoon of olive oil

Preparation

Cook elbow macaroni according to the package instructions. Drain and rinse immediately under cold water. Drizzle 1 tablespoon of olive oil over it and stir so that they don't stick to each other when you prepare the other ingredients. Meanwhile, bring a small pot of water to a boil and cook the diced carrots and potatoes for 15 minutes or until the potatoes are tender. Add in the frozen peas in the last 2 minutes. Rinse immediately under cold water and drain.

In a large bowl, put the cooked macaroni, cooked vegetables, fresh chopped dill and dill pickles and mix well. Now drizzle one tablespoon of olive oil. Add salt, mayonnaise, and thin yogurt. Toss gently until the whole mixture is well combined.

Spicy Ezme Salad

Preparation time: 40 minutes
Nutrition facts: 1 serving (230 Cal)

Ingredients (4 servings)

4 medium-sized finely chopped tomatoes peeled and without seeds

1 medium white onion, finely chopped

1-2 cloves of garlic, minced

2 medium finely chopped green bell peppers

2 finely chopped hot chilies (remove the seeds before chopping)

¼ bunch of finely chopped parsley

A few sprigs of fresh finely chopped mint leaves

1 tablespoon of lemon juice

1 tablespoon of pomegranate molasses

4 tablespoons of olive oil

½ teaspoon of hot red pepper flakes

1 teaspoon of sumac

Pita or flatbread for serving

Salt to taste

Preparation

All choppable ingredients must be chopped very finely. Combine the finely chopped tomatoes, onion, garlic, hot chilies, parsley and mint leaves in a large mixing bowl. Mix well, strain all the juices away. Now, for the dressing, mix lemon juice, pomegranate molasses and olive oil in a bowl. Stir to combine. Add salt and seasonings, mix well. Taste it and if it needs extra seasoning, add till you get preferred adjustments of all the spices. Chill salad in the refrigerator for 40 minutes and serve with warm pita/flatbread.

Turkish Tomato Cucumber Salad

Preparation Time: 25 minutes
Nutrition facts: 1 bowl (113 Cal)

Ingredients (6 servings)

6 diced Roma tomatoes

2 tablespoons of fresh lemon juice, or more to taste

¼ teaspoon of black pepper

¼ cup of finely chopped flat-leafed parsley

6 medium Persian cucumbers or 1 large English cucumber, diced, chopped into 1/2-inch pieces

1 medium white onion, chopped into 1/2-inch pieces

1 yellow or orange bell pepper, chopped into 1/2-inch pieces

3 tablespoons of extra virgin olive oil

1 teaspoon of salt

Preparations

Cut the tomatoes in half through the stem end. Cut each half in half. Starting at the opposite end stem, cut the seeds and the inner pulp out of each tomato quarter and discard. Chop tomatoes into 1/2-inch pieces. Combine the chopped tomatoes, cucumbers, onions and peppers in a medium bowl. Sprinkle with salt and stir. Drizzle the olive oil over the veggies and stir gently, but well, to coat everything with the oil. Drizzle the lemon juice on top and sprinkle with pepper and parsley. Again, stir gently but thoroughly to combine. Taste and season with more salt and pepper or lemon juice if needed. Let it sit for 17-19 minutes before serving to allow flavors to blend.

Turkish Shrimp BLT Salad

Preparation Time: 10 minutes

Cooking time: 15 minutes

Nutrition facts: 1 serving (197 Cal)

Ingredients (4 servings)

4 hard-boiled eggs, sliced

1 pound of shrimp, peeled and deveined

1/3 cup of lemon juice

2 cups of grape tomatoes, sliced in half

1 tablespoon of cumin

1/2 teaspoon of black ground pepper

1 tablespoon of paprika

1/2 teaspoon of cayenne

6 pieces of bacon, cooked and roughly chopped

8 cups of chopped romaine lettuce

1 tablespoon of dried oregano

1 tablespoon of dried cilantro

1 teaspoon of ground sumac

1/2 teaspoon of kosher salt

2/3 cup of olive oil

Preparations

In a small bowl prepare the Turkish spice mix by adding cumin, ground pepper, paprika, cayenne, oregano, cilantro, sumac and salt. Mix until ready. Now take another large mixing bowl, add the shrimp, and about 2 tablespoons of the Turkish spice mix. Toss the shrimp with the spices so that shrimps can be coated evenly with the spice mix. Preheat a skillet to a medium-high heat, pour some extra virgin olive oil on the skillet and sauté the shrimps in batches. Don't overcook the shrimps, just cook for about a minute a side or until they curl. Once all the shrimps are done, set them aside. Assembling the shrimp salad is interesting. Place two cups of romaine lettuce into a salad bowl, place the bacon pieces, sliced egg and grape tomatoes on top and add the cooked shrimps as well. Take the olive oil, lemon juice, salt and pepper and whisk them together. Pour some of the dressing on top of the salad. Repeat the process with remaining bowls.

Tomato and Walnut Salad (*Gavurdag salatasi*)

Preparation time: 10 minutes
Cooking Time: 15 minutes
Nutrition facts: 1 bowl (197 Cal)

Ingredients (4 servings)

3 finely chopped tomatoes
Half of a small onion, finely chopped
1 spring onion, finely chopped
1 garlic clove, finely chopped
2 tablespoons of flat leaf parsley, finely chopped
10 walnut halves, finely chopped
2 tablespoons of extra-virgin olive oil
1 tablespoon of fresh lemon juice
2 tablespoons of pomegranate syrup
1/2 teaspoon of sumac
1/2 teaspoon of *pul biber* (or a pinch of chili flakes)
Salt to taste
Pepper to taste
Roughly chopped walnut halves to garnish
Fresh herbs to garnish

Preparation

Take a large mixing bowl and add all the chopped ingredients except the roughly chopped walnut halves. Mix all the ingredients, add seasoning and taste. Add more olive oil, lemon juice, pomegranate syrup or spices to taste, if necessary. Serve garnished with the roughly chopped walnut halves sprinkled on top and some fresh herbs.

DIPS AND APPETIZERS

Turkish Circassian Chicken

Preparation Time: 25 minutes
Cooking Time: 60 minutes
Nutrition facts: 1 Cup (405 Cal)

Ingredients (20 servings)

1 whole chicken (5 pounds)

3 cloves of crushed garlic

1 onion

1 large carrot

5 slices of white bread (stale, crusts removed)

1 pound of crushed walnuts

3 teaspoons of paprika (sweet)

3 teaspoons of salt

1/2 teaspoon of black pepper

1 tablespoon of olive oil

Paprika and whole walnut halves

Preparation

Take a saucepan, place the chicken inside the pan and add water so that the whole chicken sinks in it. Add one whole carrot, salt, pepper and onion. Cover the saucepan and bring it to a boil. Cook until the meat leaves the bones. Meanwhile, crush the walnuts.

Once the chicken is fully cooked, turn off the flame and keep the chicken covered with lid until cooled. When the chicken is cool enough to handle, take it out of the saucepan and divide it into trips with hands, removing from bones. Discard the carrot, onion, bones and skin. Add the paprika, crushed garlic and walnuts to the shredded chicken. Mix all the ingredients well and serve garnished with a sprinkle of olive oil and walnuts.

Turkish Meze (Carrot Yogurt Dip)

Preparation Time: 15 minutes
Cooking Time: 10 minutes
Nutrition facts: 1 Cup (106 Cal)

Ingredients (6 servings)

6 medium-sized carrots, grated
1 tablespoon of olive oil
1 cup of yogurt (Turkish or Greek)
2 cloves of finely chopped garlic
6 olives, green or black
Salt to taste

Preparation

Heat the extra-virgin olive oil in a pan over medium heat and add the grated carrots. Cook for 10 minutes or until softened. Add salt and stir well. Remove from the heat and allow to cool. Place the yogurt in a medium-sized bowl, add the finely chopped garlic and cooled carrot and mix well. Pour in a serving bowl and garnish with olives and a little bit of olive oil.

Easy Turkish Lahmacun without Oven

Preparation time: 60 minutes
Cooking Time: 30 minutes
Nutrition facts: per serving (296 Cal)

Ingredients (5 servings)

Dough

2 cups of flour

1 teaspoon of instant dry yeast

1 cup of warm water

1 tablespoon of olive oil

1 1/2 teaspoons of salt

Topping

12 oz of ground beef

1 yellow onion, finely grated

4 cloves of finely chopped garlic

1 cup of finely chopped parsley

2 ripe tomatoes, finely grated

1/2 green bell pepper, grated

1 tablespoon of red pepper paste

1 tablespoon of tomato paste

1 teaspoon of paprika

1 teaspoon of hot red pepper flakes

1 teaspoon of salt

1/2 teaspoon of black pepper

1 teaspoon of cumin powder

Preparation

Mix the olive oil and warm water in a small bowl and set aside. Add the flour, instant yeast and salt in a large mixing bowl and stir to mix all the ingredients. Now pour the oil and water mixture in the flour bowl. Blend the flour well with hands until it turns into a dough, knead the dough for 14-16 minutes until it becomes soft and smooth. Sprinkle a little bit of oil on the kneaded dough, spread all around and let it sit covered for 45-50 minutes. While the dough is rising, mix all the topping ingredients in a large bowl.

Once the dough has almost doubled in size, make six equal-sized pieces from it. Roll out each piece into a very thin round flatbreads without tearing. In circles, evenly spread a thin layer of the topping over the top of each dough with your fingers, but don't press hard. Take a large non-stick skillet with a lid. Pre-heat the skillet over medium heat and add a little bit of extra-virgin olive oil with a brush all around. Place one Lahmacun in the heated skillet and cover with a lid. Cook for about 6 minutes, until the meat and dough are cooked through. As the base is thin, always check the Lahmacun as they are being cooked, to prevent them from burning. Serve them with lemon squeezed on top and add sliced onion and tomatoes.

Beetroot Dip

Preparation time: 20 minutes
Cooking time: 35 minutes
Nutrition facts: 1 serving (66 Cal)

Ingredients (4 servings)

2 tablespoons of extra-virgin olive oil

1 tablespoon of chopped mint

2 tablespoons of chopped garlic cloves

1 cup of yogurt

4 medium-sized beetroots, peeled and cubed

1 tablespoon of vinegar

Pepper to taste

Salt to taste

Preparation

Boil the beetroots in water until tender, drain the excess water. Blend the cooked beetroot, vinegar and garlic well in a blender or a food processor. In a mixing bowl add salt, pepper, olive oil and yogurt and mix with a wire whisk, until a thick creamy paste is achieved. Now add the beetroot mixture and chopped mint in the yogurt paste. Mix well and serve.

Turkish Style Brussels Sprouts

Preparation time: 10 minutes
Cooking time: 35 minutes
Nutrition facts: 1 serving (208 Cal)

Ingredients (4 servings)

1 cubanelle pepper, cut into cubes

1 tablespoon of red pepper paste

2/3 pound of Brussels sprouts

4 tablespoons of extra-virgin olive oil

8 pearl onions, divided into two pieces

2 chopped garlic cloves

2 tablespoons of tomato paste

1/3 cup of water

¼ teaspoon of sugar

1 tomato, peeled, diced

12 mushrooms, cut into halves

1 teaspoon of basil

Salt to taste

Pepper to taste

Preparation

Wash the Brussels sprouts properly in generous amounts of water, cut off the stems and remove a few outer leaves. Take a large saucepan, add water and salt. When the water comes to a boil add Brussels sprouts and cook for 3-4 minutes. Drain the water using a strainer. Heat 2 tablespoons of olive oil in a pan and add the onions, stir until the onions turn transparent and soft. Add garlic, cook one more minute, add all the remaining spices and simmer for another minute. Now add Brussels sprouts and cook for about 20 minutes. If it gets thicker, add a little bit of warm water and turn the flame off. When it cools down, add 2 tablespoons of olive oil and serve.

Stuffed Grape Leaves

Preparation time: 60 minutes

Cooking time: 120 minutes

Nutrition facts: 1 serving (66 Cal)

Ingredients (6 servings)

1 jar of grape leaves (16-ounce)

3 tablespoons of olive oil

1 medium yellow onion, finely diced

4 cloves of garlic, chopped

1 tablespoon of parsley

1 tablespoon of basil

1 ½ cups of white long-grain rice, uncooked

½ cup of raw pine nuts

8 cups of vegetable stock

2/3 cup of lemon juice

Preparation

Take out the grape leaves from the jar, wash carefully and leave to drain water. Cut them on the board and remove the stems using a sharp knife. When all the leaves are done, cover with a paper towel. Heat 2 tablespoons of olive oil in a saucepan and add the onion, garlic, parsley and basil. Stir continuously for 5-7 minutes or until the onion is soft and fragrant. Add the rice and pine nuts, stir and cook for 4-6 minutes more. Add the vegetable stock and bring to a boil. Turn the flame low for 11-14 minutes or until the rice is cooked. Add half the lemon juice, mix well and cook for 3 more minutes. When liquid is dried and the rice is cooked, remove from the flame and set aside.

Place a grape leaf inside out on a clean surface and place 1-2 tablespoons of the cooked rice mixture over the stem part of the grape leaf. Fold the leaf sides inside. Now roll the bottom over the mixture until the leaf ends so that the mixture remains invisible. Prepare all the dolmas and then place them all at the bottom of a pan one by one, while keeping the seam-side down. Sprinkle the olive oil and lemon juice over the dolma. Add the remaining vegetable stock on the dolmas and cover the pan with the lid. Simmer the dolmas for 50-60 minutes on low heat without bringing to a boil. Remove from the flame and let them rest for 30 minutes. When dolmas are cool enough, take them out on a dish with great care. Sprinkle some olive oil and lemon before serving.

Turkish Cheese Pastry

Preparation time: 15 minutes
Cooking time: 5 minutes
Nutrition facts: per serving (537 Cal)

Ingredients (6 servings)

8 thawed phyllo sheets (remember to cover with a wet cloth)
1 pound of white cheese (feta is good as well)
1/2 cup of chopped parsley
1 egg
4 tablespoons of unsalted melted butter
5 tablespoons of cream cheese
Oil

Preparation

In a mixing bowl, mix well the scrambled white cheese, egg, parsley and cream cheese. Heat the oil in a deep pan. While the oil is heating, divide phyllo sheets into triangles of equal sizes. Brush each piece with the melted butter. Place around one tablespoon of cheese mixture at the base of the dough strip but leave some space on both sides and roll up. Seal by adding the butter at the end. Repeat the same process for all the sheets. Deep fry until they turn golden brown, strain with a sieve and drain the excess oil on a paper towel. Serve with sauce.

Turkish Cacik

Preparation time: 10 minutes

Nutrition facts: 1 serving (64 Cal)

Ingredients (4 servings)

2 cups of cold plain yogurt

3 medium-sized grated cucumbers (wring out the excess water)

2 cloves of garlic, finely chopped

1 tablespoon of extra-virgin olive oil

1 cup of cold water

1/2 teaspoon of pepper

1 tablespoon of fresh mint, chopped

1/2 teaspoon of dried oregano

Preparation

Pour the olive oil and yogurt in a small mixing bowl and whisk until smooth. Add a little bit of cold water and whisk into a required thick paste. Add the grated cucumbers, chopped garlic, 1/2 teaspoon of pepper, dried oregano and chopped mint. Mix well and serve.

Turkish Zucchini Fritters (*Kabak Mucveri*)

Preparation time: 15 minutes
Cooking Time: 5 minutes
Nutrition facts: per piece (660 Cal)

Ingredients (6 servings)

4 cups of grated Zucchini (wring out the excess water)
2 carrots, grated (about 1/2 cup)
3 tablespoons of grated yellow onions
1/2 cup of white cheese (feta is good too)
1/2 cup of all-purpose flour
2 eggs
2 tablespoons of finely chopped dill/mint
1 teaspoon of salt
Olive oil for frying (as needed)

Preparation

Take a large mixing bowl, add the grated zucchini, carrots, onion and chopped dill and toss gently. Add the white cheese, salt, eggs and flour and mix well into a thick mixture. Take a frying pan and heat half a cup of oil. Pour two tablespoons of the mixture and shape fritters into round or square pieces. Fry until golden brown on each side. Crispy fritters are ready. Drain the excess oil and serve with sauce.

Chicken Salad with Mayo

Preparation Time: 2 minutes
Cooking Time: 20 minutes
Nutrition facts: 1 serving (689 Cal)

Ingredients (4 servings)

2 pieces of chicken breast, cooked, cut into medium-sized pieces

1/2 bunch of dill, washed, drained, cut into small pieces

1/4 red onion, sliced

3 fresh green onions, cut into small pieces

1/2 cup of small pickled cucumbers (cornichons), cut into small cubes

1/4 cup of walnuts, crumbled

1 cup of mayonnaise

Preparation

Mix all the ingredients in a medium-sized cup, then transfer onto a serving plate. You may garnish the salad with black olives. Serve with any kind of meal as a salad on the side. Or it can be perfect for a sandwich using the corner of a Turkish or a similar bread.

Yogurtlu Semizotu

Preparation Time: 15 minutes
Nutrition facts: 1 cup (155 Cal)

Ingredients (4 servings)

4 cups of purslane leaves, separated from the stem, washed and drained

1 tablespoon of olive oil

3 cups of plain yogurt

2 cloves of garlic, finely chopped

1/4 teaspoon of salt

1/4 teaspoon of pepper

Preparation

In a mixing bowl, add the olive oil, plain yogurt, chopped garlic, salt and pepper and whisk together using a wire whisk until it becomes a smooth and creamy mixture. Adjust the amount of salt and pepper to your taste. Add the purslane leaves and mix well until all the leaves are covered with the creamy mixture.

Crispy Sigara Borek

Preparation Time: 15 minutes
Cooking Time: 60 minutes
Nutrition facts: 1 serving (104 Cal)

Ingredients (40 servings)

2 eggs

¾ pound of crumbled feta or any white cheese

5 trimmed scallions

1/2 teaspoon of marash pepper

10 phyllo sheets

1 cup of olive oil for frying

2 tablespoons of parsley

Preparation

Mix feta cheese, eggs, scallions, marash pepper and parsley in a mixing bowl. Cut 10 phyllo sheets into 4 equal-sized pieces. Spread one small phyllo sheet on a smooth surface. Take 2 tablespoons of the cheese mixture and place it on the wider side of the small sheet while keeping the margin of folding on both sides of the mixture. Fold the extra parts inside and start rolling the sheets from the mixture side to the end. Seal the endings with the help of water. Repeat the process for all the sheets and cheese mixture and make rolls. Heat the oil in a pan and start frying the rolls in batches. Cook all the rolls until they turn golden brown. Drain the excessive oil on a paper towel. Serve with yogurt sauce.

SOUPS

Turkish Red Lentil Soup with Mint

Preparation Time: 12 minutes
Cooking Time: 35 minutes
Nutrition facts: 1 bowl (168 Cal)

Ingredients (3 servings)

1 tablespoon of butter or olive oil

1 medium onion

3 cloves of chopped garlic

1/2 cup of red lentils

1 diced carrot

1 tomato, chopped

1 teaspoon of ground cumin

1 teaspoon of paprika

1 tablespoon of fresh mint leaves, chopped

½ teaspoon of thyme or oregano

5 cups of chicken stock

1 tablespoon of tomato paste or tomato ketchup

Preparation

Heat the oil in a saucepan over medium heat. Add the onion, garlic, and a pinch of salt. Cook until translucent. Add the carrots, chopped tomatoes and the spices and mix well. Pour the tomato paste, chicken stock, red lentils, paprika and mint in the mixture and bring the soup to a boil, reduce the heat to a medium-low and continue to simmer for a few more minutes, until the lentils are tender to preference. Pour and blend the soup in a blender. Serve in bowls with garnish pepper flakes, lemon juice, a few drops of olive oil and chopped fresh mint.

Potato Soup

Preparation time: 10 minutes
Cooking Time: 20 minutes
Nutrition facts: 1 bowl (412 Cal)

Ingredients (2 servings)

2 cups of medium-sized potato cubes

2 tablespoons of fresh lemon juice

1 small finely chopped onion

1 cup of carrot cubes

1 1/2 tablespoons of all-purpose flour

½ cup of cubanelle pepper, chopped into cubes

1/2 teaspoon of fresh lemon zest

2 tablespoons of melted butter

Salt to taste

1 bay leaf

2 1/2 cups of homemade chicken stock

1/2 teaspoon of pepper

2 tablespoons of chopped parsley

Preparation

Put the melted butter in a pan and fry the onion and carrot together for 4 minutes on medium heat. Now add potato cubes, stir for 4-5 minutes. Add all-purpose flour and stir for another minute, now add the chicken stock, cubanelle pepper, salt and pepper. Let it simmer on low heat until the carrots soften. Add the parsley, lemon juice and lemon zest in. Take out the bay leaf, garnish and serve hot.

Spinach Cream Soup

Preparation Time: 2 minutes
Cooking Time: 20 minutes
Nutrition facts: 1 serving (310 Cal)

Ingredients (4 servings)

1 1/3 pounds of spinach, washed, drained
1/4 teaspoon of paprika
1/2 teaspoon of salt
1 garlic clove, chopped
2 tablespoons of plain flour
1 tablespoon of butter
1 onion, chopped
2 tablespoons of plain flour
1/4 teaspoon of pepper
4 tablespoons of heavy cream
1 garlic clove, chopped
3 cups of chicken stock
1 tablespoon of lemon juice

Preparation

In a deep saucepan, sauté the onion with the butter for 3 minutes on a medium flame. Add the chopped garlic and sauté for about one more minute. Add the plain flour, stir and slowly pour the chicken stock in it while stirring constantly, so that there are no lumps. When it starts to boil add the spinach, lemon juice, paprika, salt and pepper. Cook over medium heat for 16-19 minutes. Pour it into the blender and blend until smooth. Put a tablespoon of cream on top and serve with bread slices.

Almond Soup (*Badem Corbasi*)

Preparation Time: 2 minutes
Cooking Time: 20 minutes
Nutrition facts: 1 serving (689 Cal)

Ingredients (4 servings)

1 cup of whole milk, warm

3 cups of beef broth

1 pinch of nutmeg

3/4 cup of almonds, blanched, grounded

2 tablespoons of butter

1/3 cup of all-purpose flour

Salt to taste

Pepper to taste

Garnish

1 teaspoon of butter

1/4 cup of beef broth

1 handful of pomegranates

Preparation

Melt the butter in a medium-sized pot over medium heat. Add the flour, stir constantly so that the flour doesn't burn out. Now slowly pour the warm milk in it while stirring constantly to avoid clumps. The milk and the flour should blend very well in a smooth creamy mixture. Use an eggbeater if necessary. Then add the almonds, beef broth, nutmeg, salt and pepper. Cook for 23-25 minutes on low heat. Do not cover the pot with the lid.

Melt the butter in a small pan and add 1/4 cup of beef broth in it. When it starts bubbling, add the parsley and pour all over the soup. Place the soup into the bowls and sprinkle some pomegranates on top. Serve immediately, while still warm.

Easy Chicken Noodle Soup

Preparation Time: 15 minutes
Cooking time: 20 minutes
Nutrition facts: 1 bowl (166 Cal)

Ingredients (6 servings)

1 (12-oz) package of egg noodles

3 cups of shredded cooked chicken breast

2 medium carrots, peeled and chopped

2 stalks of celery, sliced

1 medium onion, chopped

3 garlic cloves, minced

1 leek, cleaned and chopped, whites and light green parts only

9 cups of homemade chicken broth

1 bay leaf

1 teaspoon of dried oregano

Salt to taste

A small bunch of fresh thyme

A small bunch of rosemary

Pinch of crushed red pepper flakes

Freshly ground black pepper

Preparation

In a large pot, heat oil over a medium heat, add the carrots, leek, celery, garlic, onion, and cook until all the ingredients soften. Season with salt and pepper. Add in the chicken broth, water, thyme, rosemary, bay leaf, oregano and a pinch of red pepper flakes. Bring to a boil and then add the egg noodles. Cook until the noodles are soft and done. Add the shredded chicken and simmer until warm. Make any necessary seasoning adjustments to taste and serve.

Turkish Vegetable Soup with Orzo

Preparation Time: 15 minutes
Cooking Time: 20 minutes
Nutrition facts: 1 serving (212cal)

Ingredients (4 servings)

2 tablespoons of olive oil

1 onion, finely chopped

4 cloves of chopped garlic

2 medium carrots, chopped in small pieces

1/2 cup of tomatoes, finely chopped

2 teaspoons of Turkish red pepper flakes or chili flakes

½ tablespoon of double concentrated tomato puree

1 cup of uncooked orzo pasta

2 bell peppers, deseeded and coarsely chopped

5 cups of water

Salt and ground black pepper to taste

Handful of finely chopped parsley

Juice of 1 lemon

Preparation

Heat the olive oil in a heavy, wide saucepan. Add the bell peppers, onions, garlic and carrots and cook until they start to soften up. Pour in the water, chopped tomatoes, the tomato puree and uncooked orzo seasoned with salt and black pepper. Bring it to the boil and lower the heat to simmer until orzo is cooked. Pour in the lemon juice and combine well. Remove from the heat and add freshly chopped parsley. Serve hot with Turkish red pepper flakes or chili flakes over the soup, with extra wedges of lemon.

Turkish Yogurt Soup with Chicken and Chickpeas

Preparation time: 10 minutes
Cooking Time: 40 minutes
Nutrition facts: 1 serving (599 Cal)

Ingredients (4 servings)

1/2 cup of basmati rice

4 cups of chicken stock

1 pound of skinless, boneless chicken thighs, cut into 1-inch pieces

1 cup of full-fat plain yogurt

2 tablespoons of all-purpose flour

1 can (15-ounce) of chickpeas, drained and rinsed

2 tablespoons of unsalted butter

2 teaspoons of minced garlic

2 teaspoons of sweet paprika

1/8 teaspoon of cayenne pepper

1 cup of water

3 tablespoons of finely chopped mint

Salt and freshly ground pepper

Preparation

Bring water to a boil with 1/2 a teaspoon of salt and rice in a small saucepan, cook until barely tender. Meanwhile, in a medium saucepan, bring the chicken stock to simmer, add the chicken thighs and simmer until cooked. Whisk together the yogurt, egg yolk and flour in a large pot. Slowly add the heated stock. Stir in the chickpeas, rice and the reserved chicken seasoning with salt and pepper. Melt the butter on medium heat in a small skillet. Stir in the cayenne pepper, garlic and paprika. Ladle the soup into bowls and swirl in the garlic butter. Sprinkle with mint and serve the soup with a small amount of paprika and lemon wedges.

Chicken and White Bean Spinach Soup

Preparation time: 10 minutes
Cooking Time: 25 minutes
Nutrition facts: 1 serving (225cal)

Ingredients (6 servings)

1 celery stalk

2 cups of spinach

16 ounces of cannellini beans

2 tablespoons of oil of your choice

3/4 pound of chicken breast, cut into bite-sized pieces

1 onion

4 cloves of garlic

1 teaspoon of fresh ginger, grated

2 teaspoons of coriander

1/2 teaspoon of chili powder (optional)

1/2 teaspoon of smoked paprika

1/2 teaspoon of cumin

1/2 teaspoon of turmeric

2 teaspoons of cilantros, chopped

2 teaspoons of parsley

3 packages of chicken bone broth

1 cup of crushed tomatoes

1 carrot

A pinch of red pepper flakes

1/4 teaspoon of black pepper

1 teaspoon of dried oregano

1/2 teaspoon of dried basil

1/2 cup of grated Parmesan or a similar cheese

Preparation

Heat the oil in a large pot over medium-high heat. Brown the chicken with the onions, garlic, red pepper flakes and pepper until the chicken is cooked. Add smoked paprika, coriander, chili powder, crushed tomatoes, as well as the chicken bone broth and all the remaining spices and stir well. Add in the carrot, celery and the cooked chicken and cover for some time. Add in the spinach and cannellini beans. Let it simmer until the spinach has wilted. Top each bowl with Parmesan cheese if desired and serve.

Chicken and Sweet Potato Soup

Preparation Time: 15 minutes
Cooking Time: 45 minutes
Nutrition facts: 1 serving (652 Cal)

Ingredients (5 servings)

1 1/2 cups of frozen mixed vegetables, thawed (in a colander under the cold running water)
2 cups of chicken stock
1 (6-ounce) can of mushrooms, sliced and drained
2 cups of milk, half-and-half
1 cup of celery, sliced
1 cup of onions, chopped
1/2 teaspoon of dried oregano
1/4 teaspoon of dried thyme
Salt and Pepper to taste

Preparation

In a saucepan, combine the cubed sweet potatoes and chicken stock with celery and onions. Add the dried oregano and thyme and cook over medium heat for 14-16 minutes. Add the mixed vegetables and simmer for 6 more minutes. Add the cubed chicken and mushrooms to the pot. Continue cooking over low heat for about 5 more minutes and add the milk. Taste and add salt and freshly ground black pepper to taste. Serve the soup with crackers or crusty rolls and a tossed green salad.

Turkish Tarhana Soup

Preparation Time: 30 minutes
Cooking Time: 120 minutes
Nutrition facts: 1 bowl (253 Cal)

Ingredients (6 servings)

16 ounces of plain yogurt

2 pounds of flour

1 pound of tomatoes

4 cups of water

16 ounces of chickpeas, cooked or canned, drained

1 package of active dry yeast

1 tablespoon of salt

1 teaspoon of hot red pepper flakes

1 teaspoon of black pepper

1 pound of red sweet peppers

1 pound of onions

Preparation

In a saucepan, boil the washed vegetables until softened. Drain all the excess water, add the cooked chickpeas and blend into a mixture using a blender. It will come out as a puree. If there is water in the puree, leave it in a strainer for a few minutes to drip the extra water. Put the warm vegetable puree into a large mixing bowl. Add the yogurt and mix thoroughly. Mix in the active dry yeast and spices. Add the flour very slowly and work it into the mixture entirely with your hands. Continue this process until all the flour is mixed in evenly and you have a smooth batter. Cover the top of the bowl with some cling wrap and a towel and set it in a warm place for 5 days. Check the batter every day and stir it to keep the fermentation even.

Divide the batter by placing a large spoonful on baking sheets covered with non-stick baking parchment. Leave the sheets in a dry place until the upper sides of the patties are completely dry. Flip them over and allow the other sides to dry too. After the patties look dry, you can begin to break them apart with your fingers. The centers will still be moist, so allow more time for the coarsely crumbled tarhana to dry further. Repeat the process of crumbling and drying, until the pieces are small enough to put through a food processor or a fine sieve.

Once you have a lot of fine powder, spread it out on the trays and continue to dry it, shifting the powder with your hands occasionally. In the end, you should have a fine pulse that is completely dry. It is possible to store the pulse in glass containers for more than 1 year, with no refrigeration needed. To make the soup, cook a few tablespoons of the pulse in hot milk or water until it thickens, add butter, salt and spices to taste.

Turkish Highland Meadow Soup

Preparation Time: 17 minutes
Cooking Time: 15 minutes
Nutrition facts: 1 serving (156 Cal)

Ingredients (2 servings)

1/2 cup of rice or broken rice (or substitute with 1 cup of cooked plain rice)

3 cups of water

1 large egg yolk

2 cups of plain yogurt

2 tablespoons of all-purpose flour

2 tablespoons of butter or margarine

2 tablespoons of dried mint

1 cup of water

1 teaspoon of salt

A dash of white pepper

1 teaspoon of hot red pepper flakes

Preparation

In a large saucepan boil 3 cups of water. Add rice and cook until softened. While the rice is cooking, take a small mixing bowl, add the egg yolk, flour, yogurt and 1 cup of water and beat with a wire whisk until it turns into a creamy mixture with no lumps at all. When the rice is softened enough, whisk the water and rice mixture with a wire whisk and add in the creamy mixture. Add seasonings according to your taste. Whisk the mixture continuously and add more water if the mixture is thick.

In a separate pan, melt the butter, add in the dried mint and heat for 40 seconds. Remove from the heat quickly and add the butter and mint to the soup mixture. Mix well, cook for another minute and serve hot with a fresh mint garnish.

Turkish Sweet Pea Soup

Preparation Time: 7 minutes
Cooking Time: 30 minutes
Nutrition facts: 1 tablespoon (210 Cal)

Ingredients (2 servings)

1 1/2 cups of sweet peas, frozen

1 onion, chopped

1 garlic clove, smashed with salt

1 tablespoon of butter

1/3 cup of half-half cream

2 cups of chicken stock

1 teaspoon of lemon juice

1 bay leaf

1 tablespoon of parsley, chopped

Salt to taste

Pepper to taste

Preparation

Sauté the onion with butter in a medium-sized pot for about 8 minutes over low heat. Add the garlic and stir. Then add all the ingredients above, except the cream. Bring to a boil, then turn the heat down to low to slowly cook for 28-31 minutes. Discard the bay leaf. Use a blender to blend the soup until there are no lumps in it. Pour it back into the pot. Heat it up for about 5 minutes over a very low heat. Add cream and cook for 2-3 minutes. Sprinkle some croutons on top and serve.

Turkish Vegetable Soup

Preparation Time: 25 minutes

Cooking Time: 20 minutes

Nutrition facts: 1 serving (220 Cal)

Ingredients (2 servings)

2 tablespoons of red lentil, washed

2 tablespoons of pearl barley

2 tablespoons of lemon juice

3 cups of water

1 cube of chicken bouillon

1 medium carrot, grated

1 medium potato, grated

1 small celery root, grated

Salt to taste

Preparation

In a large pan cook the water, lemon juice, barley and salt on medium heat. In the meantime, prepare all the vegetables and lentils. Add them into the pot. Cook until all the ingredients soften. Serve while hot.

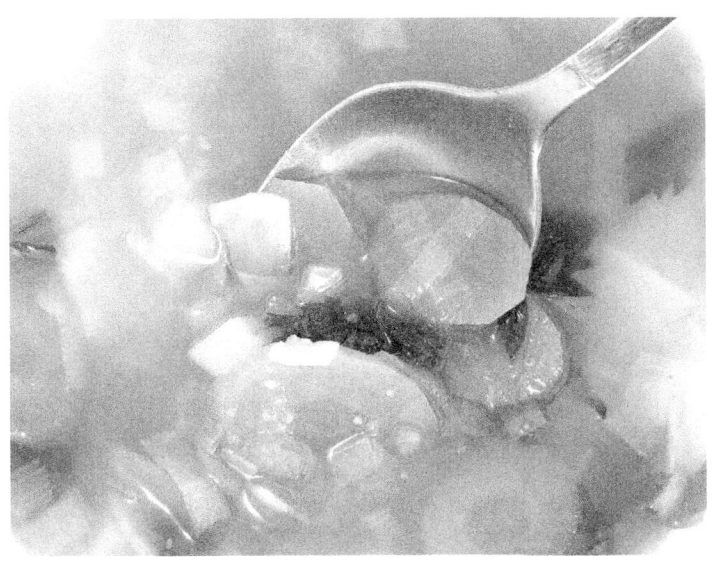

BREAKFAST

Turkish Breakfast Cookies

Preparation Time: 10 minutes
Cooking Time: 19 minutes
Nutrition facts: 1 serving (229 Cal)

Ingredients (4 servings)

2 medium ripe bananas, mashed

2 1/2 cups of whole oats, rolled

1/2 cup of peanut butter

1 egg

1/3 cup of honey

1 teaspoon of pure vanilla extract

1/2 teaspoon of ground cinnamon

1/4 teaspoon of salt

1 double dark chocolate bar, chopped

Preparation

Preheat the oven to 325 F. Take a large mixing bowl, add all the ingredients and mix well with a rubber spatula until combined. Set aside for 5 minutes. Line two large baking sheets with parchment paper. Place balls of one tablespoon of the mixture and gently give them a flatter shape with your hand. Bake for 17-19 minutes until lightly browned on the sides. Take out from the oven, let them cool for 7 minutes and transfer to a wire rack.

Turkish Menemen

Preparation Time: 5 minutes
Cooking Time: 20 minutes
Nutrition facts: 1 portion (219 Cal)

Ingredients (6 servings)

6 eggs

3 green peppers, chopped

4 cups of chopped/canned tomatoes

4 cloves of finely chopped garlic

2 green onions

3 tablespoons of olive oil

1 chopped onion

1/2 teaspoon of salt

1/4 teaspoonof black pepper

Parsley for garnish, chopped

Mint leaves for garnish

Preparation

Place a cast-iron skillet on a medium heat and pour some olive oil. Add in the chopped onion and green peppers and sauté until tender. Add the green onions, tomatoes, garlic and a pinch of salt. Let it simmer for 15-18 minutes and stir frequently until it thickens. Beat the eggs slightly and pour them on the skillet folding into the tomato mixture. Cook for about 5 to 7 minutes without much stirring. Remove from the stove before it dries out. Garnish with parsley or mint leaves.

Turkish Pancakes

Preparation Time: 5 minutes
Cooking Time: 15 minutes
Nutrition facts: 1 serving (157 Cal)

Ingredients

1 cup of yogurt

2 eggs

1 cup of oil

1 package of baking powder

1 teaspoon of salt

1 1/2 cups of all-purpose flour

Preparation

In a maxing bowl, whisk all the ingredients very well, except the flour. When the mixture is beaten enough add the flour and mix well until we get a cake like dough. Check the consistency of the batter. If thin, add a little bit of flour, mix properly until you get the desired consistency. Now grease the non-stick pan with a very little oil and cook until it gets a light brown color, flip it over and cook the other side as well. Now transfer to a tray and repeat the same process until all the dough is finished.

Turkish Style Soft Bagels (*Acma*)

Preparation Time: 20 minutes
Cooking Time: 60 minutes
Nutrition facts: 1 serving (350 Cal)

Ingredients (5 servings)

½ cup of lukewarm milk

¼ cup of lukewarm water

1 tablespoon of sugar

½ cup of light olive oil

1 pack of instant dried yeast

2 1/2 cups of all-purpose plain flour

½ teaspoon of sea salt

Glaze

1 beaten egg

1 tablespoon of sesame seeds (optional)

Preparation

Preheat the oven to 400 F. Combine the yeast with warm water in a bowl, stir well and let the yeast dissolve for a few minutes. Add the sugar, warm milk and the olive oil to the mixture, stir for the sugar to dissolve. Sift the flour in a large bowl and stir in the salt. Make a well in the middle and pour in the yeast mixture. Combine and knead the dough for a few minutes; you will get a soft dough. Cover the dough with a cling film and a tea towel and leave at a warm spot to rise for 130 minutes. The dough will double in size. Once doubled in size, divide the dough into six even-sized balls. One at a time, roll each dough ball between your palms to make it about 6 inches long. Then swirl and roll and seal the two ends together. Repeat this with the rest of the dough balls. Place the *acma* rolls on a tray on a baking paper, making sure there is a minimum of 1-inch space left between the *acma* rolls, as they expand while baking. Brush with the egg mixture and sprinkle sesame seeds over the top if you like. Bake in the preheated oven for 10 minutes. Then turn the heat down to 375 F and bake for another 10 minutes or until the *acma* has a rich, golden color.

Sujuk Sandwich (*Yengen*)

Preparation Time: 10 minutes

Cooking Time: 10 minutes

Nutrition facts: 1 serving (197 Cal)

Ingredients (8 servings)

2 slices of toast bread

2 Turkish pepperonis

2 tablespoons of butter

2 large tomatoes, washed, sliced

1 package of Mozzarella cheese, sliced

Preparation

Spread some butter on the bread. Place the cheese slices on the slice of bread, then arrange Turkish pepperoni and tomato slices on top. Cover with the second slice of bread. Preheat a grill, place the sandwich on it, toast for a few minutes until the bread gets a golden color.

Breakfast Strawberry Jam

Preparation Time: 10 minutes

Cooking Time: 17 minutes

Nutrition facts: 1 tablespoon (56 Cal)

Ingredients

1 1/3 pounds of fresh strawberries, hulled and halved

2 1/2 cups of sugar

1 lemon zest

1 large lemon juice

Preparation

Add sugar to a pan, then add a layer of fresh washed strawberries and leave in a saucepan overnight. The next morning, put the pan on a stove and cook the sugar and strawberries on a medium heat until the sugar dissolves. Remove the strawberries with a perforated spoon and place them in a separate plate. Cook the syrup for about 30-33 minutes on medium low heat. Then, add the strawberries, lemon zest and lemon juice; continue to cook over low heat for 8-12 minutes. Pour into canning jars carefully and seal. Store in a dark and cool place.

Ricotta Cheese with Green Pepper

Preparation Time: 5 minutes

Cooking Time: 5 minutes

Nutrition facts: 1 serving (179 Cal)

Ingredients (4 servings)

1 long sweet or hot green pepper, discard the seeds, sliced

2 tablespoons of extra-virgin olive oil

1/2 cup of salted Ricotta or a similar cheese

Preparation

Add 2 tablespoons of olive oil in a pan and soften the peppers for about 3 minutes on medium heat. Do not overcook. Turn the heat off, add the ricotta cheese in and toss well. Serve as a breakfast with freshly baked bread, olives and tomatoes.

Molasses Cheese

Preparation Time: 2 minutes
Cooking Time: 7 minutes
Nutrition facts: 1 serving (171 Cal)

Ingredients (2 servings)

4 oz of tongue cheese

1/2 glass of molasses

1/2 glass of Bread

Preparation

After slicing the cheese into strips, place them in a small casserole dish. Set the oven at 200 F on the grill setting and cook for 4-6 minutes, until the tongue cheese melts. When the cheese begins to melt, add half a cup of molasses on it and leave in the oven for 2 minutes before serving.

Patatesli Omlet

Preparation time: 12 minutes
Cooking time: 7 minutes
Nutrition facts: 1 serving (209 Cal)

Ingredients (2 servings)

4 eggs, beaten
1 pound of potatoes, peeled and diced
½ green pepper (optional)
3 sprigs of fresh thyme or mint, finely chopped
½ cup of grated tongue cheese
½ teaspoon of chili powder
½ teaspoon of black pepper
2 tablespoons of butter
½ capia pepper

Preparation

Melt the butter in an iron-cast pan, stir fry the diced potatoes and cook until tender. Now add the beaten eggs and cook for 2 minutes. When the eggs are half cooked add the capia and green peppers, sprinkle the chili powder and black pepper and cover with grated cheese. Cover the pan with a lid and cook for about 4 minutes. Sprinkle finely chopped mint and serve.

Slippery Roll (*Kaygana*)

Preparation time: 10 minutes
Cooking Time: 15 minutes
Nutrition facts: 1 serving (57 Cal)

Ingredients (4 servings)

1 cup of all-purpose flour

1 cup of milk

1 teaspoon of salt

4 eggs

7 sprigs of parsley

2 sprigs of green onions

1 cup of oil to cook

Preparation

Put the eggs, all-purpose flour and the milk, required for the slippery dip, into a bowl and beat well. Add finely chopped parsley and spring onions. Add salt and mix again until it turns into a mixture. Sprinkle 2 tablespoons of oil in a non-stick pan and pour the mixture into the pan like a flat bread. Cook both sides properly by turning them back and forth.

Domates Breakfast

Preparation time: 5 minutes
Cooking Time: 10 minutes
Nutrition facts: 1 serving (Cal 170)

Ingredients (2 servings)

1 large tomato, sliced

1 tablespoon of extra-virgin olive oil

1 teaspoon of butter

3 slices of black peppered roast beef

2 tablespoons of white cheese

1 teaspoon of dry basil

Salt to taste

Preparation

Add the extra-virgin olive oil to a pan and arrange the tomato slices on the surface. Cook for 2 minutes. When one side has cooked properly, turn over to the other side and add more butter. Cut the roast beef slices into pieces with hands and adjust these pieces to the blank sections of the pan. Slices of black peppered roast meat can be optional. Add the cheese and when it melts, remove the pan from the flame. Sprinkle the dry basil, salt and serve.

Tomato and Cheese Panini

Preparation Time: 5 minutes
Cooking Time: 5 minutes
Nutrition facts: 1 serving (210 Cal)

Ingredients (2 servings)

2 buns

1 tablespoon of butter

2 slices of mozzarella or a similar cheese

1 thinly sliced tomato

2 green peppers, sliced

½ teaspoon of dried thyme

½ teaspoon of chili

Preparation

Preheat the panini presser. Apply butter on both sides of the buns, inside and outside. Place the mozzarella slices in the buns. Sprinkle thyme and chili over them. Place a tomato slice and pepper slices inside and bring both sides together. Place them in a panini presser and cook for 5 minutes. Serve with tomato sauce.

Turkish Borek with Cheese and Herbs

Preparation time: 15 minutes
Cooking Time: 45 minutes
Nutrition facts: 1 slice (66 Cal)

Ingredients (2 servings)

4 phyllo sheets

2 cups of yogurt

¼ cup of olive oil

4 eggs

Filling and Topping

2 chopped leeks

½ cup of chopped parsley

½ cup of crumbled feta cheese

¼ cup of parmesan/mozzarella

3 chopped green onions

¼ cup of fresh dill/mint, chopped

2 tablespoons of nigella seeds

Preparation

Preheat the oven to 350 F. Combine all the filling ingredients, except the nigella seeds in a mixing bowl. Mix well and set aside. Take another bowl and mix the yogurt, eggs and olive oil and make a mixture. Take a baking sheet (suitable size is 14x16 inches) and grease it lightly with oil. Layer the first phyllo sheet in the baking sheet with the sides overhanging. Brush its top roughly with the egg and yogurt mixture. Remove the overhanging parts nicely and layer them on already a mixture coated layer. Brush the top of the phyllo sheet pieces with the mixture. Repeating the step, place the second phyllo sheet in the same way. Brush with the mixture. Again, remove its overhanging parts, place the pieces on top and brush with the mixture.

Spread the filling evenly on top of this layer. Place the third phyllo sheet over the filling, brush with the mixture. Again, remove the overhanging pieces, place them on top of the third layer. Brush with the mixture. Finally, place the fourth phyllo sheet and brush it with the mixture. Remove the overhanging pieces, put them on the last layer and drizzle all the rest of the egg and yogurt mixture on top. Spread it evenly using a brush. Slice the *borek* in squares and sprinkle it with nigella seeds. Bake it for 40-45 minutes or until its top is golden. Remove from the oven, cover it with a large clean towel and let it cool. Covering with a paper towel will keep the *borek* tender.

Soganli Yumurta

Preparation Time: 3 minutes
Cooking Time: 7 minutes
Nutrition facts: 1 serving (65 Cal)

Ingredients (2 servings)

2 eggs
2 large onions, chopped
2 tablespoons of extra-virgin olive oil
Salt to taste
Pepper to taste

Sauce
1 tablespoon of butter
1 teaspoon of red or cayenne pepper

Preparation

Sauté the onions with the olive oil in a large skillet. Make two holes for the eggs between the onions. Break the eggs in and cover with the lid. Cook on low heat until the eggs are done. Melt the butter in a small pan and add pepper. When it starts to bubble up, pour over the eggs and onions. Serve this dish while still hot.

Classic Turkish Breakfast

Preparation Time: 2 minutes

Cooking Time: 15 minutes

Nutrition facts: 1 serving (80 Cal)

Ingredients

1 hard-boiled egg

1 green pepper, sliced

1 tomato, sliced

1 cucumber, sliced

5 Black olives

4 green olives

1 dried apricot

¼ pound of cured meat (salami for example)

¼ pound of a good quality salty white cheese

¼ pound of mozzarella

Sumac, salt and pepper

Parsley, for garnish

Preparation

Cut the hard-boiled egg in quarters and place it in the center of the plate. Arrange the remaining items on the plate around the egg. Garnish the egg with sumac, salt and pepper and sprinkle the entire plate with flatleaf parsley.

MAIN DISHES

Pasta with Yogurt Sauce

Preparation Time: 15 minutes
Cooking Time: 35 minutes
Nutrition facts: 1 serving (400 Cal)

Ingredients (2 servings)

2 servings of pasta
1 1/2 tablespoons of butter
Salt

Sauce
1/2 cup of yogurt
2 garlic cloves, smashed with salt

Preparation

Boil the pasta according to the instructions on the package, drain. Melt the butter in a pot. Toss the pasta and salt it. Place the pasta on a serving plate. Mix the yogurt and garlic cloves and pour it all over the pasta. Serve it with tomato and cucumber slices.

Turkish-Style Lamb (*Kavurma*)

Preparation Time: 12 minutes
Cooking Time: 180 minutes
Nutrition facts: 1 serving (577 Cal)

Ingredients (6 servings)

3 pounds of boneless lamb roast (or boneless leg and thigh of lamb)

1/4 pound of lamb or tail fat

2 teaspoons of salt

Preparation

In a saucepan, add the lamb meat and fat after cutting them into bite-sized cubes. Add the salt and spread it with your hands. Turn the heat high and let the bottom of the pan begin to sizzle. Cover the pan with a lid and turn down the heat to a low flame. Leave the pan to simmer very gently for several hours. Occasionally turn the meat over with a wooden spoon. The meat is ready when it is falling apart and has darkened in color and there is no liquid left, except the melted fat. Serve the hot *kavurma* with a side dish of rice.

Turkish Stuffed Bulgur Meatball (*Ichli Kofte*)

Preparation Time: 40 minutes
Cooking time: 20 minutes
Nutrition facts: 1 serving (550 Cal)

Ingredients

Dough

14 oz of bulgur, well-grounded

4 oz of semolina

4 oz of flour

2 cups of water, boiling

1 egg

1 tablespoon of pepper paste

1 teaspoon of salt

½ teaspoon of black pepper

½ teaspoon of red pepper flakes

1 teaspoon of cumin

Meat filling

9 oz of ground beef, medium-fat

9 oz of onions

3 oz of coarsely chopped walnuts

2 tablespoons of butter

1 teaspoon of salt

½ teaspoon of black pepper

1 teaspoon of allspice

1 teaspoon of dry mint

1 tablespoon of red pepper paste

1 ½ cups of olive oil (for frying)

Preparation

In a large mixing bowl, add the grated onions, bulgur, black pepper, red hot pepper powder, sliced potatoes, extra lean ground beef, salt, wet bread slices, semolina and 1 egg. Combine all the ingredients well and knead them for 25 minutes to form a bulgur dough. It's good to add water constantly while kneading, because the dough gets dry fast.

Put the beef in a deep non-stick pan, add salt and cover the lid. Let it cook for about 11 minutes. Add the oil and diced onions and cook for another 6 minutes. Add the other seasonings - black pepper, red pepper powder and pepper paste and stir well. Turn off the flame and set aside to cool.

Wet your hands with water and take walnut-sized pieces of the bulgur dough. Roll them into balls. Make holes in the balls by using your thumb in a circular motion. Put the meat filling and the crushed walnuts inside the space, close the bulgur dough ball and make an oval shape. Continue until all the filling is gone. Add a generous amount of oil in a deep-frying pan and fry the bulgur balls until all the sides are golden brown. Extra strain oil using a paper towel.

Kiymali Ispanak

Preparation Time: 25 minutes
Cooking Time: 30 minutes
Nutrition facts: 1 tablespoon (234 Cal)

Ingredients (2 servings)

1 small tomato, peeled, cut in small cubes
1 teaspoon of red pepper paste
3 tablespoons of crushed tomato, in can
1 pound of fresh baby spinach, washed, drained, coarsely chopped
1 medium-sized onion, finely chopped
2 tablespoons of extra-virgin olive oil
6 oz of medium ground beef
1 tablespoon of butter
2 tablespoons of rice, rinsed
Salt to taste
Pepper to taste

Garlic Yogurt Sauce
1/2 cup of plain Turkish yogurt, room temperature
2 cloves of garlic, mashed with salt

Preparation

Sauté the onion with olive oil and butter for about 3 minutes on a medium heat. Add the ground beef, salt and pepper and stir. Cook together until the color of the ground beef turns light brown. Add the rice, tomato, red pepper paste and crushed tomatoes, stir again. Place the spinach all over and close the lid. Cook on a medium heat until the rice is tender without adding water. Place the dish in a serving plate and pour a couple of spoons of garlic yogurt sauce over the top.

Sweet Chicken with Cherry Sauce

Preparation Time: 2 minutes

Cooking Time: 20 minutes

Nutrition facts: 1 serving (689 Cal)

Ingredients (4 servings)

1 whole chicken

2 tablespoons of butter

1 lemon, cut in 4

1 small onion, peeled

1 teaspoon of oregano

Salt to taste

Pepper to taste

Cherry Sauce

1 cup of cherry compote juice, in a jar-in light syrup

1 1/2 cups of cherries

1 tablespoon of butter, unsalted

4 tablespoons of sugar

1 tablespoon of honey

1 teaspoon of cinnamon

1 tablespoon of corn starch

1 /4 cup of sliced almonds, roasted

Preparation

Wash the chicken and dry it with a paper towel. Season the inside and outside of the chicken with salt and pepper. Also season the inside with oregano and place the lemon wedges and onion in it. Spread the butter all over the chicken with your hand. Place the chicken in an oven dish, cover with aluminum foil. Preheat the oven and cook the prepared chicken for 28-32 minutes. Remove the aluminum foil; reduce the heat to 350 F and cook for another 60 minutes. Let the chicken sit for 12 minutes and then cut in four.

Cherry Sauce

Place the honey, sugar, cinnamon and corn starch in a small pot over medium heat. Slowly add 1 cup of cherry compote juice and stir constantly to avoid lumps. When it gets thicker, add in the cherries and butter. Cook for another minute and turn the heat off. Place the baked chicken pieces on serving plates. Pour the cherry sauce over the chicken, sprinkle some roasted almonds and serve.

Turkish Beef and Veal Kebab

Preparation Time: 45 minutes

Cooking Time: 10 minutes

Nutrition facts: 1 serving (380 Cal)

Ingredients (4 servings)

10 oz of ground beef

½ pound of ground veal

½ teaspoon of red pepper flakes

1 onion, finely chopped

2 tablespoons of melted butter

3 tablespoons of extra-virgin olive oil

1 teaspoon of tomato paste

1 teaspoon of salt

Preparation

In a mixing bowl, add all the ingredients and mix with hands, so that all the ingredients get combined in a mixture form. Wrap the mixture tightly with plastic foil. Keep this foiled mixture in the refrigerator for about 40 minutes. Preheat a large non-stick grill pan over a medium flame. Take the meat mixture out of the fridge. Shape them into 2-inch logs. Cook for 9-11 minutes. Turn the kebabs occasionally so that all the sides are cooked adequately. Serve immediately with your favorite greens.

Turkish Beef Kebab

Preparation Time: 65 minutes
Cooking Time: 15 minutes
Nutrition facts: 1 serving (476 Cal)

Ingredients (4 servings)
1 pound of ground beef
1 large onion, chopped
½ cup of red bell pepper
½ cup of yellow bell pepper
6 cloves of garlic, chopped
½ cup of parsley
1 tablespoon of black pepper powder
½ tablespoon of red chili, crushed
1 tablespoon of all ground spices
2 tablespoons of butter
1 tomato, sliced
2 finely chopped green chilies
Salt to taste

Preparation
In a large mixing bowl, add salt, black pepper, all ground spices powder, crushed red chilies, chopped onion, green and yellow bell peppers, garlic, green chilies and ground beef and mix until well combined. Marinate for at least 45 minutes.

In a non-stick pan, add butter and let it melt. Add the marinated ground beef mixture, spread it in the pan evenly and cook on a medium-low heat for 5 minutes. Add the chopped tomatoes and green chilies and cook. When one side is golden, flip carefully and cook the other side as well, on low flame. Cut into equal-sized square or rectangle pieces with the help of a kitchen cutter.

Turkish Beef Tava

Preparation time: 15 minutes
Cooking time: 60 minutes
Nutrition facts: 1 serving (599 Cal)

Ingredients (4 servings)

2 pounds of beef stew meat, cut into 1/2 inch pieces
1 medium-sized green bell paper, chopped
2 fresh tomatoes, chopped
1 small red onion, chopped
1 pack of shredded Mozzarella cheese
1 green chili pepper, chopped
½ teaspoon of chili paste
1 tablespoon of olive oil
1 jar of mushrooms, drained

Preparation

Heat the oven at 350 F. Lightly grease a medium casserole dish. Put a tablespoon of olive oil in a skillet and place the ground beef into the skillet. Cook the beef for 23 minutes or until all the juices run out. Now add the mushrooms in the greased casserole dish, add the tomatoes, red onion, green pepper, green chili and cooked ground beef. Drizzle with 1 tablespoon of olive oil, and top with mozzarella cheese. Bake for about 40 minutes in the preheated oven, until bubbly and the cheese has melted or until the meat is no longer pink. Serve hot with flatbread or wrapped in a pita.

Turkish Bulgur and Vegetable Pilaf

Preparation time: 15 minutes
Cooking time: 20 minutes
Nutrition facts: 1 serving (401 Cal)

Ingredients (4 servings)

2 tablespoons of margarine or butter
2 tablespoons of oil
1 medium onion, grated
1 large tomato, grated
1 small green bell pepper, chopped
2 cups of coarse bulgur
1/2 teaspoon of black pepper
2 tablespoons of tomato paste
2 teaspoons of sugar
4 cups of chicken broth
Fresh or grilled pepper and parsley (for garnishing)
Salt to taste

Preparation

Melt the butter with the oil in a shallow pan. Fry the grated onion until tender, but don't let it turn brown. Add the grated tomato with juice and grated pepper and continue to fry to reduce the liquid. Add bulgur and stir well to combine. Add the salt, pepper, tomato paste, sugar and chicken broth. Bring the mixture to a boil, reduce the heat to low and cover it. Let the bulgur simmer gently until all the liquid has been absorbed. Set aside to cool down. Before serving, gently stir the pilaf to make sure all the ingredients are mixed well. Garnish with grilled pepper or parsley.

Turkish Okra and Tomato with Olive Oil

Preparation time: 75 minutes
Cooking time: 30 minutes
Nutrition facts: 1 serving (180 Cal)

Ingredients (8 servings)

2 ¼ pounds of young okra

Lemon Juice of ½ a lemon

1 large onion, diced

3 tablespoons of sugar

1/3 cup of virgin olive oil

2 tablespoons of olive oil

1 large tomato, peeled and chopped

3 teaspoons of salt

1/2 teaspoon of black pepper

Preparation

Wash the frozen okra thoroughly and soak them in 1 cup of vinegar for 27-32 minutes. Rewash them to remove all the vinegar. Heat two tablespoons of olive oil in a saucepan and fry the onions until reduced. Add the okra and tomatoes. Add the lemon juice and spices and turn the mixture gently with a wooden spoon. Add the sugar and water. Bring it to a boil and let the okra simmer gently. As the vegetables release their juice, the amount of liquid in the pan will increase, so simmer them until the water is gone. Turn off the heat and let the pan cool to a room temperature. Transfer the okra to a serving plate and sprinkle the 1/3 cup of olive oil over the top of the dish.

Turkish Style Kofte in Garlic Yogurt Sauce

Preparation Time: 35 minutes
Cooking Time: 10 minutes
Nutrition facts: 1 serving (989 Cal)

Ingredients (6 servings)

½ tablespoon of black peppercorns

6 cloves

¼ cup of roasted chickpeas

1 pound of beef mince

3 tablespoons of fried onions

4 green chilies, chopped

1 small onion, chopped

½ cup of fresh coriander

1 tablespoon of ground spices powder

¼ tablespoon of turmeric powder

1 tablespoon of ginger garlic paste

1 tablespoon of mustard oil

2 tablespoons of cooking oil

1 tablespoon of coriander powder

2 cups of yogurt

3 garlic cloves

Salt to taste

Red chili powder to taste

Preparation

In a spice mixer, add all the spices and roasted chickpeas and blend to make a fine powder. In a chopper, add the ground spices, beef mince, fried onions, green chilies, fresh onion, coriander, ground spices powder, salt, red chili powder, turmeric powder, ginger garlic paste and mustard oil and chop well.

Wet your hands with oil, take 2 tablespoons of the mixture and make around 15 meatballs. Place the prepared meatballs in a pot. Cover and steam the meatballs on a low flame for about 15 minutes. Keep turning so that they get golden all around. Add water, cover and cook on a low flame for 10 minutes. Add the cooking oil, coriander and turmeric powder, red chili powder and salt and mix well. Now in a small jug, add the yogurt, salt and garlic and whisk well. Serve with potato fries, garlic yogurt and fresh coriander.

Pureed Fish Roe (*Tararna*)

Preparation time: 30 minutes
Cooking time: 40 minutes

Ingredients (5 servings)
4 slices of day-old white bread, crusts removed
1 small onion, chopped
1 (6-ounce) jar of mullet roe
1 1/2 cups of virgin olive oil
1/4 cup of lemon juice
Chopped fresh parsley
Olives
Salad greens
Pita bread, cut into triangles

Preparation
Soak the bread slices in water briefly and squeeze the excess water out. Place the bread, onion and roe in a food processor fitted with a metal blade. Process on low speed until they're mixed well. Slowly add the olive oil and lemon juice; continue processing on low speed for about 2 minutes, until the mixture is a thick paste. Transfer it to a serving bowl, cover and refrigerate.

Izmir Meatballs in Tomato Sauce
(*Izmir Koftesi*)

Preparation time: 25 minutes
Cooking time: 45 minutes

Ingredients (4 servings)

4 slices of day-old white bread, crusts removed

2 pounds of lean ground lamb or beef

½ of a small Spanish onion, grated (1/4 cup)

4 garlic cloves, minced

2 eggs

1 teaspoon of paprika

1 tablespoon of ground sumac

1/4 cup of finely chopped fresh Italian parsley

Salt and fresh ground black pepper

1/4 cup of virgin olive oil

2 tablespoons of unsalted butter

1 tablespoon of tomato paste

3 large tomatoes, peeled, seeded and finely chopped (2 cups)

2 cups of water

Salt and freshly ground black pepper

2 medium Italian green peppers, seeded and cut diagonally into slices

Preparation

Heat the oven to 350 F. Soak the bread in cold water briefly and squeeze the excess water out. Combine the ground lamb, bread, garlic, onion, paprika, eggs, cumin and parsley in a large bowl. Season with salt and pepper. With moistened hands, mix the ingredients for 3 minutes. Keep a bowl of warm water nearby to wet your hands while working. Shape the meat mixture into 15 oval balls.

Heat the oil in a large skillet over high heat, add the kofta balls and lightly brown the meat all over for 6 minutes. Place the koftas in an ovenproof dish and set them aside.

Melt the butter in a small saucepan. Stir in the tomato paste. Add the tomatoes and lamb stock and season with salt and pepper. Bring the mixture to a boil, stirring. Pour this sauce over the koftas. Arrange the green peppers on top. Cover the dish and bake for 35-45 minutes.

Zesty Lamb Chops with Couscous

Preparation time: 30 minutes
Cooking time: 55 minutes
Nutrition facts: 1 serving (683 Cal)

Ingredients (8 servings)

2 tablespoons of extra-virgin olive oil

8 lamb chops or cutlets

Grated zest and juice of 3 lemons

1 lemon, sliced

1 onion, chopped

12 oz of whole-wheat couscous

1 oz of currants

4 oz of olives, roughly chopped

5 oz of baby leaf spinach

A handful of chopped mixed herbs

Preparation

Prepare the couscous following the directions mentioned on the box. Heat the oil in a thick based frying pan over a medium-high heat. Season the lamb with the lemon slices, salt and pepper and cook for 4-6 minutes. Turn the other side and cook until the lamb is tender. Take a small bowl, mix the onion and lemon juice and set aside. Once the lamb is cooked, transfer it to a large cooking pot. Add water and boil on high heat. Add in the remaining lemon juice, most of the olives, lemon zest and currants. Take off of the heat and stir in the couscous, spinach and most of the herbs. Serve the chops and the couscous garnished with onion, the remaining spices and lemon zest.

Turkish Shrimp and Vegetable Clay Pot Casserole

Preparation Time: 20 minutes
Cooking Time: 15 minutes
Nutrition facts: 1 serving (476 Cal)

Ingredients (4 servings)

1 1/3 pounds of shrimps
1 tablespoon of tomato paste
2 green bell peppers
1 cup of small button mushrooms, fresh
3 Hungarian wax peppers
1 onion, chopped
3 garlic cloves, chopped
3 tablespoons of olive oil
3 ripe tomatoes
1 teaspoon of salt
¼ teaspoon of black pepper
¼ teaspoon of hot red pepper flakes
1 cup of grated yellow cheese

Preparation

Fill a saucepan with water. Add one teaspoon of salt, boil and add the shrimps. Boil for 2 minutes. Rinse the shrimps and run them in cold water. Clean and chop the green peppers. Clean the mushrooms. Fry the onions and garlic in a saucepan in the heated olive oil until they soften and become transparent. Add the green peppers. Add the chopped mushrooms, tomatoes, tomato paste and spices and stir until the mixture dries out. Add the cooked shrimps. Transfer the mixture to a large pot or an oven-proof dish. Generously cover with cheese. Cook the casserole in the oven, set until the cheese has melted, is bubbly and brown. Remove and immediately serve while it's still hot.

Lamb Casserole with Prunes

Preparation Time: 15 minutes
Cooking Time: 120 minutes
Nutrition facts: 1 serving (533 Cal)

Ingredients (4 servings)

1 tablespoon of light olive oil

1 1/3 pounds of lamb neck, cut into bite-sized pieces

1 tablespoon of cumin seeds, crushed in a pestle and mortar

1 teaspoon of ground allspice

2 onions, sliced

5 cloves of garlic, crushed

3 cups of chicken stock

4 oz of soft dried prunes, roughly chopped

3 tablespoons of pomegranate molasses to taste

A bunch of coriander, chopped

2 oz of shelled unsalted pistachios, roughly chopped

Steamed couscous to serve

Preparation

Preheat the oven to 375 F. Take a heavy-based casserole with a lid and add oil, set over medium heat, add the lamb and brown all over. Cook all the lamb in batches, then remove from the casserole and set aside on a plate. Add onions to the casserole and cook for 9-11 minutes, stirring, until lightly browned. Add the allspice, garlic and cumin seeds and cook for another 2 minutes. Return the lamb and any resting juices to the casserole, then add the stock. Add the seasonings, bring to a boil and add the prunes. Cover with the lid, place in the oven and cook for 100 minutes or until the meat is tender. Add the pomegranate molasses, season, then sprinkle with coriander and pistachios and serve with couscous.

Turkish Muhammara

Preparation Time: 15 minutes
Cooking Time: 40 minutes
Nutrition facts: 1 serving (147 Cal)

Ingredients (2 servings)

4 large red or green peppers
1 garlic clove, roughly chopped
1 red chili, deseeded and finely sliced
1 teaspoon of cumin seeds
4 oz of fresh white breadcrumbs
Juice of ½ a lemon
4 tablespoons of pomegranate molasses
3 oz of walnuts, finely chopped
Extra-virgin olive oil
Pomegranate seeds to garnish

Preparation

Roast the peppers over a grill on an open flame for 16-22 minutes, or until tender and charred all over. When the roasting is done, set aside to let it cool and remove the skin once cooled. Crush the garlic and chili in a large pestle and mortar with a good pinch of salt. Add the cumin seeds and whizz again. Chop the peppers roughly and add to the mortar with the breadcrumbs, lemon juice and two tablespoons of pomegranate molasses. Work together until well combined with some texture. Add the walnuts to the mortar along with a good pinch of black pepper. Add enough extra-virgin olive oil for it to loosen, then taste and tweak the seasonings. Spoon onto a serving plate, drizzle with the rest of the pomegranate molasses and a little more oil, then serve sprinkled with the pomegranate seeds and pul biber.

Quick Chicken Kebabs

Preparation Time: 60 minutes
Cooking Time: 20 minutes
Nutrition facts: 1 serving (524 Cal)

Ingredients (4 servings)

1 1/3 pounds of free-range skinless, boneless chicken thighs

½ of a large cucumber, deseeded and sliced into half-moons

4 oz of thick Greek yogurt

1 tablespoon of sweet smoked paprika

1 teaspoon of ground cumin

4 flatbreads or tortilla wraps

7 oz of cherry tomatoes, halved

2 little gem lettuces, torn

Pickled green chilies to serve

Preparation

Mix the paprika, yogurt, cumin and garlic in a large ceramic or glass mixing bowl and season with salt and pepper. Transfer a generous spoonful to another small bowl and set aside. Toss the chicken in the large bowl, marinade with the yogurt, then set aside for at least 40 minutes. Heat the grill to a medium-high. Put the marinated chicken thighs on a lined grill pan and grill for 9-11 minutes. Turn and grill for 6-7 minutes, or until cooked through and charred in places. Transfer to a board and chop it roughly. Heat the flatbreads under the grill for 1-2 minutes, then divide the chicken, cucumber, tomatoes, and lettuce equally among the wraps. Add a spoonful of cold water to the reserved bowl of yogurt mixture to thin it slightly and make a dressing. Drizzle some into the wraps, then roll up and serve with the pickled green chilies on the side.

Koylu Kebab

Preparation Time: 20 minutes
Cooking time: 80 minutes
Nutrition facts: 1 serving (211 Cal)

Ingredients (6 servings)

1 whole chicken (3 ½ pounds)
1 red bell pepper
1 green bell pepper
2 large onions
4 garlic cloves, crushed
1 ½ tablespoons of tomato paste
1 cup of extra virgin olive oil
3 1/3 pounds of potatoes, peeled
3 medium tomatoes
Juice of 2 lemons
1 tablespoon of dried oregano
Salt and ground pepper

Preparation

Set the oven to 375 F. Cut the chicken into 10 pieces. Wash it and drain well with a paper towel. Season with salt and pepper and place the pieces in a deep large tray. Cut the potatoes and peppers into big chunks and add them to the tray together with the crushed garlic cloves. Cut the tomatoes into 4 pieces and place them in the tray. Dilute the tomato paste in 2 cups of hot water and pour it in together with the lemon juice and the olive oil. Add the oregano, season with salt and pepper and give the contents of the tray a good stir. Cover the tray with aluminum foil and cook in the oven for 85-95 minutes. Uncover the tray and cook for another 18 minutes to give your chicken a nice golden-brown color.

Broccoli and Carrot Tabbouleh

Preparation Time: 15 minutes
Cooking Time: 30 Minutes
Nutrition facts: 1 bowl (431 Cal)

Ingredients (4 servings)

1 small onion, finely diced
1 small broccoli, broken into florets and whizzed in a food processor
2 medium-sized grated carrots
11 oz of cooked quinoa
4 oz of unroasted shelled pistachios
Olive oil for frying

Dressing

2.5 oz of extra-virgin olive oil
Grated zest and juice of 1 lemon
½ oz of fresh chopped chives
1 garlic clove, finely chopped
½ teaspoon of Dijon mustard
1 teaspoon of maple syrup

Preparation

Take a small mixing bowl to add the olive oil, chopped chives, lemon juice and lemon zest, garlic, mustard, maple syrup and a pinch of salt and whisk all the ingredients well. Set aside. Heat a half cup of the oil in a medium-sized pan over a gentle heat. Sauté the onion with a pinch of salt for 4-6 minutes, until soft and translucent. Add the carrots and cook for a few minutes. Add the broccoli to the pan and cook for 1-3 minutes more, or until both the carrots and broccoli are tender, occasionally stirring to prevent burning. Once tender, transfer the vegs to a serving dish, pour the dressing over the warm vegetables and mix. Stir in the quinoa and nuts, season to taste.

Turkish Cauliflower Stew

Preparation Time: 15 minutes
Cooking Time: 20 minutes
Nutrition facts: 1 serving (97 Cal)

Ingredients (4 servings)

1 medium-sized cauliflower, broken into florets
2 carrots, peeled and sliced
1 onion, peeled and sliced into half-moons
1 tablespoon of Turkish *salca*
2 tablespoons of tomato paste
1 tablespoon of olive oil
1 teaspoon of chili flakes or paprika
A handful of chopped flat leaf parsley
Salt and pepper to taste

Preparation

Heat the olive oil in a deep pan, add the onion and sauté until it starts to sweat or become transparent. Add your carrots and stir them around. Keep the flame low and gently sauté for 4-6 minutes, or until your carrot begins to cook and soften. Add salt, pepper or chili flakes. Meanwhile, put the tomato paste and *salca* into a cup and add boiling water or vegetable stock. Stir until the *salca* dissolves. Add the cauliflower to the pan along with the dissolved *salca*. Now add enough hot water or stock to cover the cauliflower florets. Stir everything, bring to a boil and then simmer until your cauliflower is soft. Top with chopped parsley.

Turkish Roasted Lamb

Preparation Time: 15 minutes
Cooking Time: 10 minutes
Nutrition facts: 1 serving (206 Cal)

Ingredients (6 servings)

1 leg of lamb (drumstick and thigh portions)
5 bay leaves
3 fresh rosemary sprigs
1/4 cup of olive oil
Juice of ½ lemon
1 teaspoon of salt
1/2 teaspoon of black pepper
1/2 cup of hot water

Preparation

Preheat your oven to 285 F. Clean the lamb from unnecessary fat. Place the lamb in a shallow metal oven roasting tray. In a mixing bowl, whisk together the spices, olive oil and lemon juice. Pour the mixture over the lamb, massaging it into the meat for several minutes. Add the bay leaves and rosemary sprigs. Place the uncovered tray in the oven. Let the lamb cook slowly at a low temperature for 85-95 minutes. Meat will release its fat and juices and then reabsorb them as it cooks. After the first 30 minutes, turn the pieces of lamb over. Repeat this two more times during the cooking process. When the cooking time is over, pour 1/2 a cup of hot water over the meat, then close the roasting pan completely with aluminum foil. Turn up the oven temperature to 365 F and leave the meat to roast for at least another hour. After about 60 minutes, remove the pan from the oven and let it rest for 5 minutes. Remove the foil. The meat should be very tender and fall cleanly off the bones. Remove all the bones and discard them. Remove the bay leaves and rosemary.

Ground Beef Stuffed Grape Leaves

Preparation Time: 15 minutes
Cooking Time: 180 minutes
Nutrition facts: 1 serving (162 Cal)

Ingredients (8 servings)

30 grapevine leaves

13 oz of ground lamb or beef

1 cup of water to cook the stuffed wine leaves

2 small onions, finely chopped

4 oz of long-grain rice, rinsed and drained

1 bunch of fresh dill and flat-leaf parsley, finely chopped

1 teaspoon of dried mint

3 tablespoons of olive oil

6 tablespoons of plain yogurt to serve

Salt and ground pepper to taste

Preparation

In a bowl, mix the ground meat with the onions, rice, spices and herbs. Add a tablespoon of olive oil and knead thoroughly. Place a vine leaf onto a working surface and add some filling in the center. Cover the filling with the leaf sides, fold in the sides and roll it tightly into a log. Do not overfill the leaves to stop the filling from oozing out. Layer the rolled logs tightly in a deep broad pan, with the seam side facing down. Combine the water with the remaining olive oil and pour over the rolls. Add more water if needed, to ensure that the top layer of the vine leaf rolls is covered. Cover the rolls with a heavy plate and cook over a moderate flame until it starts to boil. Then lower the heat and cook for 35-45 minutes, until it's cooked through. Serve hot, with a spoonful of yogurt.

Beef Stew with Creamy Cheese Eggplant

Preparation time: 20 minutes
Cooking Time: 60 minutes
Nutrition facts: 1 serving (232 Cal)

Ingredients (6 servings)

1 pound of top ground beef
1/3 cup of grated Romano cheese
1 grated onion
4 cups of fire-roasted eggplants
1 tomato, grated
½ teaspoon of pepper
½ teaspoon of sugar
Freshly ground white pepper to taste
2 heaping tablespoons of all-purpose flour
4 cups of milk
1 teaspoon of salt
3 tablespoons of butter

Preparation

Take a saucepan and add the meat, chopped tomatoes and onions. Make sure to squeeze the extra juice from them. Add the salt, paper and sugar and mix all the ingredients well. The flame should be high at the start to lock the moisture, after that, lower the heat and cover the saucepan. Cook for 50-60 minutes or until the meat is tender and the onions and tomatoes come in an excellent thin sauce-like consistency. Stir occasionally. Meanwhile, mash the eggplants. They can be roasted on flame and the flesh can be extracted if you are using fresh eggplants. If you are using canned eggplants, put the flesh in a strainer and wash off the entire canned flavor from the eggplant. Rinse off thoroughly to get rid of all the extra moisture.

Take another saucepan and add the butter and half a teaspoon of oil. Add the flour and don't let this mixture get burnt. After 2 minutes, when the flour is tossed thoroughly and no lumps can be seen, add milk in it. Stir constantly to avoid forming lumps. Mix the mixture well, leaving no lumps behind. Add the salt, paper and garlic in the sauce and let the sauce cook on low flame. Don't boil it. Add the eggplants and cheese at this stage. Stir constantly so that the eggplants and cheese melt completely, leaving no chunks of eggplant in the sauce.

Put the pan on the lowest flame possible, cover and let the sauce cook for about 6-8 minutes. Uncover the pan and give it a final stir before switching off the flame. Then cover the bottom of your serving platter with the sauce. Garnish with the grated cheese and fresh rosemary sprigs just before serving.

Midye Dolma

Preparation Time: 15 minutes
Cooking Time: 50 minutes
Nutrition facts: 1 serving (172 Cal)

Ingredients

1 teaspoon of fresh mint
1 cup of cracked rice
2 teaspoons of dill
24 black mussels, scrubbed, beards removed
½ cup of pine nuts
½ cup of olive oil
2 garlic cloves
1 teaspoon of ground pimento
3 onions
14 oz of diced canned tomatoes
½ cup of raisins
Parsley for garnishing

Preparation

Wash the rice and let it soak in a bowl for 20 minutes, then rinse and drain. Take another bowl, add lukewarm water and soak the mussels in it for 8-11 minutes. Slice the onions into granular shapes and chop the garlic. Add the olive oil in a pan and fry the onions and garlic in the pan together. Add the pine nuts and pimento on low heat until it gets golden brown.

Add the rice and tomatoes to a saucepan and cook for 2 minutes. Add seasoning according to your taste. Pour water to cover the rice, bring it to a boil and cover. Cook for 14-16 minutes or until the liquid is absorbed. Pour the rice into a bowl and garnish with mint and dill. Let it cool for 7 minutes.

Hold each mussel by its narrow end with the pointed edge facing outwards and remove the breads. Create a small gap by squeezing the shells gently from the opposite edges to the broader ends. Open the shells slightly by inserting a small sharp knife in-between the shells and take precautions not to break them. Cut the part where the mollusk is attached to the shell through the foot. Stuff a vast amount of rice mixture into each mussel and then close the shells. Take a pan for mussels. Add ½ a cup of boiling water, cover it and let it boil for minutes until the mussels are tender. Take them out and let the mussels cool in a separate pan. Garnish with chopped parsley and sprinkles of lemon juice.

Nigel Slater with Lemon Potatoes

Preparation Time: 15 minutes
Cooking Time: 40 minutes
Nutrition facts: 1 serving (322 Cal)

Ingredients (2 servings)

For the Potatoes

12 anchovy fillets

1 cup of vegetable stock

4 tablespoons of olive oil

1 pound of fleshed potatoes, sliced lengthwise into 6 pieces each

1 large lemon

For the Fish

Whole sea bass, cleaned but left on the bone

4 tablespoons of olive oil

1 teaspoon of oregano

Preparation

Preheat the oven to 400 F. Heat the olive oil in a roasting tin, put the potatoes in and let them color on both sides. Leave them alone for several minutes in between the stirrings. Make sure that they are pale gold on both sides. Cut a lemon into 8 pieces, add in the potato tray and sprinkle with black pepper. Lay the fish on top of the potatoes, brush with a little bit of olive oil, then add the herbs and a mild seasoning of salt and black pepper. Bake in the oven for 22-27 minutes, the fish will easily slide from the bone in big pieces.

Fresh Salmon Chowder

Preparation Time: 10 minutes
Cooking Time: 40 minutes
Nutrition facts: 1 serving (490 Cal)

Ingredients (8 servings)

12 to 16 ounces of fresh salmon, diced (or canned flaked salmon)

1 cup of frozen peas, thawed

2 cups of half-and-half (or whole milk)

2 cups of cheddar cheese, shredded

3 tablespoons of butter

1/2 cup of celery, diced

1/2 cup of carrots, diced

1/4 cup of onions, finely chopped

2 tablespoons of all-purpose flour

1 tablespoon of parsley, chopped

Freshly ground black pepper

1 2/3 cups of chicken broth

2 cups of diced potatoes

Salt

Preparation

Heat the butter over medium-low heat. Add the onions, celery and carrots and sauté for 5 to 7 minutes, or until the celery is tender. Stir occasionally and then add flour. Mix well. Stir in the chicken broth and add the potatoes. Bring to a simmer, frequently stirring, for 16 to 19 minutes, or until the potatoes and carrots are tender. Add the salmon and peas. Stirring, cook for 2 to 4 minutes, or until the peas are tender. Add the milk, along with cheese and parsley. Taste test and season with salt and pepper to taste. Cook while stirring, until the cheese has melted and the soup has just begun to bubble.

Shish Taouk

Preparation Time: 10 minutes
Cooking Time: 17 minutes
Nutrition facts: 1 serving (306 Cal)

Ingredients (8 servings)

2 pounds of cubed chicken breast

1/4 teaspoon of cumin

1/2 teaspoon of pepper

1/8 teaspoon of cayenne

2 cloves of garlic, finely chopped

3 tablespoons of lemon juice

1 tablespoon of olive oil

Preparation

Combine all the ingredients and allow the chicken to marinate for at least 130 minutes, covered, in the refrigerator. Place the chicken on skewers (about 5 pieces on each) and grill for 16 minutes or until done. Turn the skewers during the cooking process. Serve shish taouk with rice, bread and salad.

Adana Kebab

Preparation Time: 17 minutes
Cooking Time: 14 minutes
Nutrition facts: 1 serving (213 Cal)

Ingredients (4 servings)

1 pound of ground lamb
1/4 teaspoon of ground black pepper
1/4 teaspoon of red pepper flakes
2 tablespoons of ice-cold water
1 1/2 teaspoons of ground cumin, divided
1 1/2 teaspoons of ground sumac, divided
1 small onion, peeled and minced
4 cloves of garlic, peeled and minced
1/2 teaspoon of salt
4 metal or wooden skewers, soaked in water

Preparation

Combine the ground lamb, minced garlic and onion, 1 teaspoon of ground cumin, 1 teaspoon of ground sumac, red pepper flakes, salt, ground black pepper and ice water in a large bowl. Knead the mixture by hand until it turns tacky and starts sticking to the sides of the bowl. Place in the refrigerator for 27-32 minutes to chill. Wet your hands and place a quarter of the lamb mixture onto each skewer. Use a 1-ounce scoop to form balls and thread them onto the skewer, then mash them together. Grill the kebabs, for approximately 12 minutes, until they are well charred on both sides. Combine the remaining 1/2 teaspoons of ground cumin and sumac and sprinkle them over the kebabs while they are cooking. Serve with warm pita breads with sliced red onions, tomatoes and diced cucumbers.

Chicken and Sausage Jambalaya

Preparation Time: 15 minutes
Cooking Time: 35 minutes
Nutrition facts: 1 serving (299 Cal)

Ingredients (6 servings)

1 medium tomato, chopped

2 tablespoons of Cajun seasoning

2 bay leaves

1 cup of long grain rice

1 ¾ cups of chicken stock

1 tablespoon of vegetable oil

1 pound of boneless skinless chicken breast halves, cut in 1-inch cubes

1 pound of andouille sausage, sliced 1/4-inch thick

1 medium red onion, chopped

1 medium green bell pepper, chopped

1 rib of celery, chopped

1 medium tomato, chopped

Preparation

Heat the oil in a large, heavy skillet on a medium-high heat. Add the chicken and sausage, cook and stir for 6 minutes. Remove from the skillet and pour off the excess oil. Add the celery, onion and bell pepper, cook and mix on a medium heat until the onion is softened. Stir in the tomato, Cajun seasoning and bay leaves.

Return the chicken and sausage to the skillet. Add the rice and stock and bring it to a boil. Reduce the heat to a low setting; cover and cook for 25 minutes or until the rice is tender. Stir occasionally. Remove the bay leaves before serving.

Turkish Chicken and Rice Pie

Preparation Time: 45 minutes

Cooking Time: 120 minutes

Nutrition facts: 1 serving (590 Cal)

Ingredients (5 servings)

3 ½ tablespoons of unsalted butter

2 tablespoons of extra-virgin olive oil

2 medium onions, peeled and sliced thinly

½ teaspoon of dried mint

1 large carrot, peeled and chopped

1 medium onion, peeled and quartered

2 stalks of celery, peeled and chopped

3 sprigs of fresh flat leaf parsley

6 whole black peppercorns

6 whole cloves

Ground black pepper

½ teaspoon of dried mint

1 cup of long grain white rice

1/3 cup of blanched almonds

3 sheets of phyllo pastry dough

1 lightly beaten egg

2 tablespoons of unsalted butter, melted

Salt to taste

Preparation

Put the chicken in a large saucepan or along with the bay leaves, onion, celery, carrot, parsley, peppercorns and cloves. Add cold water and bring to a boil over medium heat. Lower the heat, cover with a lid and simmer for 80-95 minutes until cooked. Remove from the heat and let it cool for 40 minutes in the pan. Transfer the cooled chicken to the cutting board. Remove all the meat and shred it into a large bowl. Strain the chicken stock and set 2 cups of it aside in a measuring cup.

Heat the butter and olive oil in a pan over medium heat and sauté the onions and mint for 6 minutes, or until softened. Add the rice and almonds and cook, stirring, for 5 minutes. Add the reserved chicken stock and season generously with sea salt and freshly ground black pepper. Bring to a boil, then lower the heat, cover with a lid, and simmer for 16 minutes, or until the rice is cooked and has absorbed most of the liquid. Let it cool for 12 minutes.

Preheat the oven to 400 F. Add the shredded chicken to the cooled pilaf and mix well.

Whisk the egg and butter together in a small bowl. Place the phyllo sheets on a flat surface, cut them in half and cover with a damp cloth to prevent them from drying out. Place a piece of phyllo inside each greased cariole mold, pushing them into the sides and leaving the excess phyllo hanging over the edges. Spoon the pilaf into each lined mold, pressing it in tightly. Fold the excess phyllo over the top and brush it with the egg wash.

Place the molds in a roasting pan and bake in the preheated oven for 22 minutes or until the top is golden brown. Let them cool for 5 minutes before carefully inverting the molds onto plates.

Turkish Liver and Onions

Preparation Time: 15 minutes
Cooking Time: 45 minutes
Nutrition facts: 1 serving (704 Cal)

Ingredients (4 servings)

1 pound of fresh calf or lamb liver
1 teaspoon of salt
1 teaspoon of black pepper
6 teaspoons of flour
1/2 teaspoon of paprika
4 tablespoons of butter
1/3 cup of olive oil or vegetable oil for frying
1 large red onion
1 teaspoon of ground sumac
1/3 cup of chopped parsley

Preparation

Wash the liver cubes with a generous amount of cold water in order to wash out the extra blood. Drain the extra water and dry the liver cubes with a paper towel. Put the paprika, salt, black pepper and flour in a mixing bowl and mix well, add liver cubes and mix so that all the cubes are covered with the flour mixture.

In a large skillet, heat the olive oil and butter together and add all the liver cubes at once, now adjust them into the skillet so that they can cook properly. Turn the sides when one side is cooked properly. Do this for all the sides. Adjust all the cubes accordingly, if needed. Meanwhile, take the onion slices and toss them with parsley, salt and ground sumac. When the liver is cooked, turn the flame off and transfer it in a serving tray.

Nazik Lamb

Preparation Time: 20 minutes
Cooking Time: 30 minutes
Nutrition facts: 1 serving (213Cal)

Ingredients (4 servings)

Meat Topping

1/2 pound of lamb or beef

1 tomato

2 tablespoons of vegetable oil

1 teaspoon of red pepper paste, or tomato paste

1 teaspoon of salt

1 sweet green pepper

2 tablespoons of butter

1/2 teaspoon of black pepper

3 tablespoons of water

Chopped parsley

Eggplant Mash

4 medium Japanese eggplants

1 cup of yogurt (plain or Greek)

2 cloves of garlic

1 teaspoon of salt

1/2 teaspoon of black pepper

Preparation

Wash the eggplants and pierce each one in several places with a thin skewer or a toothpick. Lay them on the grill and leave them to roast. As the flesh inside softens, the eggplants will collapse. Turn them to cook evenly on all sides. Cut the tomato and pepper in quarters and lay the pieces on the grill next to the eggplants. Turn them as they become brown.

Chop the lamb into small, bite-sized chunks about the size of the kidney beans. In a skillet, melt two tablespoons of butter. Add the lamb and sauté until tender. Let it release its juice. As the lamb cooks, add salt, pepper, vegetable oil and pepper paste and cover the pan. Reduce the heat to low and let the lamb simmer gently until very tender. Add a few teaspoons of water if needed. The eggplants should be soft by now. Remove them from the grill. While they're still hot, run a knife down the length of each eggplant to open it up. Use a spoon to scoop out the warm, soft flesh.

In a bowl, mix the plain yogurt, salt and pepper. To serve, cover the bottom of a platter with the eggplant and yogurt mash while it's still warm. Spoon the meat over the top and drizzle the oil and pan juices over it. Add more melted butter if needed. Garnish with the grilled pepper, tomato pieces and parsley.

Rice Pilaf with Chicken and Chickpeas

Preparation Time: 35 minutes
Cooking Time: 35 minutes
Nutrition facts: 1 serving (757 Cal)

Ingredients (4 servings)
1 1/2 cups of short grain rice
2 cups of chicken broth
1 cup of water
2 teaspoons of salt
½ teaspoon of black pepper
1 onion
1 (12 oz.) can of chickpeas
2 tablespoons of butter
2 tablespoons of olive oil
1 carrot

Preparation

Place half of the whole chicken in a pot and add water until it sinks into the water. Add the carrot and onion, cover the lid, let it simmer, and cook for 28-32 minutes. Remove from the flame and set aside to cool. Remove all the meat from the bones and discard the bones, skin, onion and carrot. Drain and rinse the chickpeas and set them aside. In a large, shallow pan, melt the butter together with the oil. Add the rice and work the oils through all the grains with a wooden spoon. On low heat, continue to 'fry' the dry rice for a few minutes. Add the chickpeas, chicken broth, water and spices. Bring the liquid to a boil, then reduce the heat and cover. Let the rice simmer very gently on low heat until all the liquid is absorbed. Turn off the heat. Open the top of the pan and arrange the chicken pieces over the top of the cooked rice. Do this quickly as you don't want to lose too much steam. Replace the cover and let the rice continue to steam for about another 12 minutes. Using a large bowl as a mold, arrange the chicken pieces at the bottom and up the sides of the bowl. Using a wooden spoon, fill the bowl with the hot rice and gently pack it down to make it firm. When the bowl is full, turn it upside down on your serving plate.

Stuffed Zucchini Flowers

Preparation Time: 60 minutes
Cooking Time: 35 minutes
Nutrition facts: 1 serving (304 Cal)

Ingredients (12 servings)

30 fresh zucchini flowers
1 large onion, finely chopped
1/2 cup of olive oil
1/3 cup of dried currants
1/3 cup of pine nuts
1 large bunch of fresh dill weed
2 cups of short-grain white rice
3 teaspoons of salt
1/2 teaspoon of black pepper
3 teaspoons of cinnamon
2 teaspoons of allspice
2 tablespoons of sugar

Preparation

Do not wash the flowers as they are too delicate, and it will cause their petals to stick together. As these flowers are to be stuffed, remove all leaf or green parts that are present. To make the stuffing, take a saucepan and add the onions in some olive oil. Sauté until the onions are slightly pink. Add the pine nuts in the onions and sauté them as well. Add all the dry ingredients and mix them well. Add water and reduce the flame so that the mixture is cooked thoroughly, leaving a fragrant smell behind. Once the stuffing is completely cooled, it is ready to be stuffed in flowers. Use a spoon to stuff the flowers and use the back of the spoon to move the petals inwards so that the stuffing is completely covered. Do not overstuff the flowers.

Leave some space for the rice to expand and cook. After stuffing the flowers, place them in a shallow pan. Add water in the pan to cover the flowers, add a teaspoon of olive oil and salt in the water. Boil the water on high flame, then reduce the heat and cover the pan so that the flowers can be cooked thoroughly. When the water is reduced completely, remove the pan from the heat and let the flowers cook in the steam. Cover the pan with a paper or a towel if needed. When the flowers are cooked thoroughly, they become easier to handle and can be easily removed from the pan.

Turkish-Style Stuffed Peppers (*Biber Dolması*)

Preparation Time: 30 minutes
Cooking Time: 35 minutes
Nutrition facts: 1 serving (284 Cal)

Ingredients (12 servings)

1/2 cup of olive oil

3 teaspoons of cinnamon

12 small green peppers

2 cups of water

1 medium tomato, grated

2 teaspoons of allspice

1 large bunch of dill weed

2/3 cup of dried currants (or dark raisins)

2/3 cup of pine nuts

2 cups of white rice (short grain)

2 tablespoons of sugar

1 large onion, finely diced

1/2 teaspoon of black pepper

3 teaspoons of salt

Preparation

Add the olive oil to the pan and put it on a medium flame. After that, add the rice and the onions and fry them in the olive oil until they are soft. Add the pine nuts and let them change their color to brown along with the onions. Add all the dry ingredients and mix them well. Wash the peppers and clean out all the seeds and white membranes inside the peppers.

Remove the stems by pressing your thumb gently down the base of the branch and create a perfect hole for stuffing. Pour some water in it with the grated tomato and boil it. Put a lid on it and let it cook until the water is absorbed. Let your filling cool down and arrange the empty peppers at the bottom of a saucepan. Make sure to arrange the peppers side by side, leaving no space between them. Now add your rice mixture into the peppers, but don't overfill. Once the peppers are filled, cover the opening of each with a square of a tomato, skin side up. Add water, so that the peppers are half dipped into it. Add two tablespoons of olive oil and some extra salt in the water. Boil the water and turn the heat low. The peppers must simmer gently with the lid on and let most of the water get absorbed. Remove the saucepan and let it cool down. Once the peppers are cool, they become firm, so you can remove them one by one easily, without damaging any of them.

Turkish Eggplant and Ground Beef Casserole

Preparation Time: 30 minutes
Cooking Time: 95 minutes
Nutrition facts: 1 serving (740 Cal)

Ingredients (8 servings)

1 onion

1 sweet pepper

1 large tomato

5 eggplants

1/2 teaspoon of allspice

3 large tomatoes

1/4 teaspoon of black pepper

1/2 teaspoon of oregano

3 tablespoons of flour

1 tablespoon of tomato paste

2 cups of vegetable oil (for frying)

3 cups of milk

1 tablespoon of olive oil

3 tablespoons of butter or margarine

1/2 teaspoon of sugar

1 pound of ground lean beef

1 cup of grated mild, yellow cheese

1 teaspoon of salt

Sweet red pepper strips or slices, or green pepper

Preparation

Peel the eggplants and slice them into pieces. The size of the slice should be ¼ inches thick. Grate the tomato and slice the green pepper into rings. Chop some onions, add 1 tablespoon of olive oil in it and let it change its color to light brown. Add the green peppers and ground beef and let it fry until it turns brown. Add the tomato, tomato paste and all the spices in it. In a separate saucepan, grate the other tomato and put it on the flame. Add sugar, salt, tomato paste, pepper and oregano and cook this sauce for 9-12 minutes, then remove it from the stove. Take out the eggplants from the water and dry them with a towel. Fry them in oil of your choice and let them turn their color to brown. After frying, drain the excess oil with a paper tissue.

Get a baking tray and line up these fried eggplants at its bottom, leaving no gaps between them. Spread the tomato sauce over the eggplants nicely, then cover this sauce with the meat mixture. Now take a separate pan and melt some butter in it, add the flour and mix with the help of a spoon. Add the milk and the seasonings and stir that sauce continuously to make it vigorous. Béchamel sauce is ready if it has a consistency of a pudding. Pour the béchamel sauce over the meat in such a way that it covers the whole platter from upside down. Add some grated cheese over the top of everything, put the casserole in the oven and heat it on 360 F until the top turns golden brown. When it is baked, remove the casserole from the oven and let it cool down for 7 minutes, then cut it into pieces of your desired shapes.

Turkish Iskender Kebab

Preparation Time: 12 minutes
Cooking Time: 10 minutes
Nutrition facts: 1 serving (814 Cal)

Ingredients (4 servings)

2 pounds of rib-eye steak or lamb or beef tenderloin

3 tablespoons of olive oil

2 teaspoons of dried oregano

2 teaspoons of red pepper flakes

Salt and freshly ground black pepper to taste

Sauce

2 tablespoons of concentrated tomato paste

2 tablespoons of olive oil

2 cups of water

2 green pointy or bell peppers, deseeded and sliced

Salt and freshly ground black pepper to taste

3 medium tomatoes, cut into wedges

1 tablespoon of red pepper paste (optional)

1 tablespoon of tomato paste and red (optional)

2 cups of plain yogurt to serve

Preparation

Grate the onions to get their juice without anything solid left of the onions. Slice the meat into thin pieces so that it can be cooked easily. Make sure to marinate the meat a day before you have to cook it, by doing so, the spices will be well marinated. Get a large bowl and combine the onion juice, oregano, olive oil, red chili flakes, salt and freshly ground pepper in it and mix them well. Combine this marination with the meat and dip it in properly. Cover the bowl and leave it in the fridge overnight. Get a saucepan, add some olive oil into it. Add the tomato paste, red pepper paste and red chili flakes into it. Add salt and freshly ground black pepper and combine all these spices very well. Add some water and bring to a boil, then let it simmer for 9-12 minutes. Slice the pita bread into slices and warm it for minutes, then place it on a platter. Get a saucepan, drizzle some olive oil on it and cook the meat slices on high heat. Now sauté the sliced tomatoes and peppers in another pan. On a plate, place warm sliced pita bread and the cooked meat with the sautéed vegetables.

DESSERTS

Turkish Sweet Churros

Preparation Time: 5 minutes
Cooking Time: 30 minutes
Nutrition facts: 1 serving (537 Cal)

Ingredients (6 servings)

Dough

2 ½ cups of all-purpose flour

2 cups of water

2 oz of butter

1 teaspoon of sugar

1 pinch of salt

3 eggs

1 tablespoon of semolina

1 tablespoon of starch

2 cups of sunflower oil to fry

Syrup

1 tablespoon of lemon juice

4 cups of water

4 cups of sugar

Preparation

Heat the water in a saucepan and melt the unsalted butter in hot water. Add the flour and stir fast on a medium heat. Stir until it becomes soft and turns into a non-sticky dough. Remove from the flame, transfer the dough to another bowl and let it cool. While the dough is cooling down, prepare the sugar syrup. Pour 4 cups of water and sugar in a large pot and boil over a medium heat. When it starts to boil, add the lemon juice, turn the stove off and set aside. Take a cooled dough mixing bowl and begin mixing the eggs with a mixer. Add the semolina and starch and start adding your eggs gradually. Mix well until it becomes smooth. Fill your piping bag with the dough. Pipe the dough into frying oil. When they have fully browned, take them out and directly transfer them into the sweet syrup. After 2 minutes, take them out of the syrup onto the plate.

Semolina Halva with Pine Nuts

Preparation Time: 15 minutes
Cooking Time: 32 minutes
Nutrition facts: 1 serving (640 Cal)

Ingredients (8 servings)

3 ½ cups of semolina

1 ¾ cups of unsalted butter

2 ¼ cups of sugar

3 ½ cups of milk

1/3 cup of pine nuts

Cinnamon for garnish

Mixed nuts for garnish

Preparation

In a medium pot, combine the milk and sugar, stir occasionally and let it scald. Once it is done, remove it from the flame. In another saucepan, melt the butter, add semolina and pine nuts, and stir the semolina continuously until it is appropriately mixed with the butter. Heat the mixture with constant stirring until it turns golden brown, and make sure not to let the mixture burn. When it is done, turn the flame off, pour the hot milk mixture and mix well, cover it with a lid and let it settle. Once the semolina mixture absorbs all the liquid, the halva is cool enough to handle. Crumble the mixture with fingers or a wooden spoon before serving, garnish with cinnamon and mixed nuts.

Kunefe Sweet Cheese Pastry without Oven

Preparation Time: 15 minutes
Cooking time: 40 minutes
Nutrition facts: 1 serving (508 Cal)

Ingredients (4 servings)

Kunefe

2 cups of shredded raw kadaifi dough

4 oz of butter

1 tablespoon of extra butter to brush the pans

7 oz of unsalted mozzarella cheese

1 tablespoon of ground pistachios for topping

Syrup

1 cup of water

1 cup of sugar

1 slice of lemon

1/4 teaspoon of rosewater (optional)

Preparation

Preheat the oven to 375 F. Pour the water, sugar and a slice of lemon in a saucepan and bring to a boil. Simmer for 15-16 minutes on a medium flame until it gets a little thicker texture. Remove from the flame and set aside to cool. Melt the butter and bring it to room temperature. Place the shredded kadaifi dough in a large bowl and add the butter, coat the kadaifi dough evenly. Take a 9-inch pan, brush the bottom, spread half of the butter coated dough evenly on the surface and press with your hands. Toss the shredded unsalted cheese over evenly. Cover the cheese with the remaining kadaifi noodles and press on them with your hands. Cook it over the lowest heat on the stove, until the bottom is golden. When one side is done flip the dessert and cook the other side until golden as well. Repeat the same for the leftover kadaifi dough. Pour our cold syrup over as soon as you remove them from the flame. Let them absorb the syrup and serve immediately with ground pistachios on top while it's still hot.

Tulumba

Preparation time: 35 minutes

Cooking Time: 15 minutes

Nutrition facts: 1 serving (637 Cal)

Ingredients (24 servings)

3 eggs

3 tablespoons of semolina

2 tablespoons of cornstarch

2 tablespoons of butter

2 tablespoons of sugar

2 cups of water

2 1/2 cups of all-purpose flour

Vegetable oil for frying

Groundnuts for garnishing

Syrup

3 cups of sugar

3 1/2 cups of water

1 1/2 tablespoons of lemon juice

Preparation

Stir 3 cups of sugar and 3 ½ cups of water together in a saucepan on medium heat. Bring the mixture to a boil and stir until the sugar is dissolved. Let the syrup simmer gently for 14-16 minutes on low heat. Add the lemon juice and simmer for 1 more minute. Turn off the heat and set aside to let it cool. In a saucepan, add 2 cups of water, butter and 2 tablespoons of sugar and stir continuously until the butter has melted on low heat. Stir in the flour using a wooden spoon until a loose dough is formed. When the dough begins to collect around the spoon, remove the pan from the heat and let it cool. Add one egg at a time into the dough and stir them in with the wooden spoon. Add the semolina and cornstarch, combining well with the wooden spoon. Transfer the batter to a pastry bag fitted with a star tip. Pour about 3-4 inches of oil into a deep-frying pan and heat to 350 F. Once the oil is hot, squeeze out small lines of dough directly into the hot oil. Use a strainer or spoon to turn the pieces over and around, so that they brown evenly. When the tulumba are evenly browned, remove them from the oil and drain on paper towels. Add them to the cool syrup and let them soak it up. Arrange the syrupy sweets on a serving plate and garnish with ground nuts.

Fake Chicken Breast Pudding

Preparation Time: 15 minutes

Cooking Time: 45 minutes

Nutrition facts: 1 serving (300 Cal)

Ingredients (9 servings)

1 ½ cups of sugar

1 tablespoon of vanilla extract

2 ½ tablespoons of unsweetened butter

1 cup of all-purpose flour

1 liter of milk

½ cup of shredded coconut

Preparation

In a saucepan, melt the butter and add flour. Stir constantly and evenly. Once the butter and flour are combined, add the sugar and continue to stir. Add the milk and vanilla extract while still mixing. To avoid forming lumps in the milk, keep stirring constantly. Use a wooden spoon or a wire whisk. Continue stirring until the mixture thickens. Pour the mixture in a serving dish and sprinkle the coconut on top. Refrigerate and serve cold.

Gullac

Preparation Time: 5 minutes
Cooking Time: 10 minutes
Nutrition facts: 1 serving (250 Cal)

Ingredients (10 servings)

10 gullac sheets of phyllo dough
2 liters of milk
1 pound of sugar
1 tablespoon of rosewater
1 tablespoon of crumbled walnuts to garnish
1 tablespoon of ground pistachios to garnish
8 strawberries to garnish, sliced

Preparation

Pour the milk into a saucepan together with 1 tablespoon of rosewater and sugar and heat until the sugar has dissolved. Stir it occasionally and don't let the milk boil. Take a gullac sheet and place it in a wide medium depth pan. Pour a generous amount of milk over the sheet and let it absorb the milk. Place the second gullac sheet and pour the warm milk again. Repeat this with three more sheets. After the fifth one, spread the crumbled walnuts on it. Then again place the remaining five gullac sheets one by one and wet each one f them with milk. When you are done with the tenth one, pour the rest of the milk on it. Now the sheets begin to rise, do not touch them. Cover it with a stretch film and put it in the refrigerator for at least 140 minutes. Garnish before serving.

Kazandibi

Preparation Time: 10 minutes
Cooking Time: 40 minutes
Nutrition facts: 1 serving (210 Cal)

Ingredients (12 servings)

6 cups of milk

4 tablespoons of powdered sugar

1 teaspoon of cinnamon

3 tablespoons of rice flour

3 tablespoons of cornstarch

1 cup of granulated sugar

1 tablespoon of butter

Preparation

In a deep saucepan, combine the milk, granulated sugar, rice flour and cornstarch. Mix the mixture with a whisk until smooth and cook on the stove until thick. Add the butter, mix and let it melt in the dessert's temperature. Cover the entire surface of a greased baking sheet with a mixture of powdered sugar and cinnamon. Separate two scoops of the custard in equal amounts. Put the tray on the stove and pour one half of the mixture in it. When the burning process is over, pour the remaining custard into the tray. Fix it with a spatula. To raise the consistency, put in the fridge. Cut the dessert you have cooled into long thin slices and roll them up with a spatula.

Berry Trifle

Preparation Time: 15 minutes
Cooking Time: 30 minutes
Nutrition facts: 1 serving (713 Cal)

Ingredients (8 servings)

9 oz of mini jam Swiss roll, cut into pieces
3,5 oz of framboise liqueur
1 1/3 pounds of mixed berries (strawberry/raspberry/blueberry)
1 pound of fresh vanilla custard
12 oz of double cream
9 oz of cream cheese
2 tablespoons of rosewater
1 teaspoon of vanilla essence
2 oz of plain chocolate
Icing sugar for dusting
7 oz of sliced Turkish delight, use before serving (optional)

Preparation

Make the jelly following the instructions given on the package. Take a large trifle glass tray and pour the jelly mixture in it. Add the berries before refrigerating the jelly to set. Refrigerate for 4 hours or until set. Mix the cream cheese and vanilla custard together to make it smoother. Pour the custard and cream cheese mixture on top of the berry mixed jelly. Place the mini jam rolls on top of the custard mixture. In a large mixing bowl, beat the cream, sugar, vanilla essence and rosewater until softened. Sprinkle with the Turkish delight and mixed berries. Dust some icing sugar and serve.

Katmer

Preparation Time: 12 minutes

Cooking time: 10 minutes

Nutrition facts: 1 serving (503 Cal)

Ingredients (8 servings)

4 tablespoons of melted butter

4 oz of unsalted pistachios, finely ground

5 oz of k*aymak*

4 phyllo dough sheets

2 tablespoons of granulated sugar

Preparation

Take two sheets, brush the phyllo sheets with melted butter and place them on top of each other. Place small blobs of *kaymak* on top of the two-layered buttered phyllo sheets and sprinkle granulated sugar and pistachios on the *kaymak* layer evenly. Fold the four corners of the phyllo sheets inside in an envelope-like shape. Take the melted butter and brush the envelope with the melted butter again. Repeat the same for the rest 2 sheets. Brush the surface of a non-stick pan with butter and heat on a medium flame. After the butter melts, put the prepared envelope sheets into the pan and fry each side for 1.5-2 minutes. When one side is done flip the envelope on the other side and fry for another 1.5-2 minutes. After both sides have a light golden color, take them out of the pan and put them on a serving plate. Cut into pieces, sprinkle the finely ground pistachios and serve hot.

Turkish Baked Rice Pudding

Preparation Time: 20 minutes
Cooking Time: 20 minutes
Nutrition facts: 1 serving (496 Cal)

Ingredients (4 Servings)

2 tablespoons of cornstarch
1 egg yolk, beaten with 3 tablespoons of milk
½ cup of uncooked rice
4 ¾ cups of whole milk
1 cup of sugar
1 teaspoon of vanilla extract

Preparation

Preheat the oven to 350 F. Wash the rice and place it in a large saucepan with enough water to cover it by about ½ inch. Bring it to a boil and reduce the heat. Let the rice simmer gently for 4-6 minutes or until the rice is soft. Add 3 ¾ cups of milk, sugar and vanilla extract to the rice. Bring the mixture to a boil. Reduce the heat and let it boil very gently for about 11 minutes. Using a whisk, mix together the remaining 1 cup of the milk and the cornstarch, in a small bowl, until smooth. While stirring, gradually pour this mixture into the rice. Turn up the heat and continue stirring the pudding until scalding.

When the pudding thickens, continue to stir and cook for an additional 2 minutes. Remove from the heat and fill the small, ovenproof dessert cups, clay cups, or disposable aluminum pudding cups with the hot mixture. Using a spoon, drizzle a small amount of the egg yolk and milk mixture into the center of each dessert cup. With the back of the spoon, use a light, circular motion to swirl the egg yolk from the center to the edges so that it spreads evenly over the top of each cup. Bake the pudding cups until the tops are nicely browned, for about 20 minutes. Let the cups cool at room temperature and then refrigerate them for several hours before serving.

Turkish Noah's Ark Pudding

Preparation Time: 60 minutes
Cooking Time: 60 minutes
Nutrition facts: 1 serving (634 Cal)

Ingredients (6 servings)

8 dried apricots, cut into chunks

8 dried figs, cut into chunks

3 cups of uncooked whole grain wheat or barley

1 1/2 cups of canned chickpeas, rinsed and drained

3 cups of sugar

2 cinnamon sticks

1 1/2 cups of canned navy beans, rinsed and drained

1/4 cup of uncooked rice

3 tablespoons of dried currants

Preparation

The night before preparation, put the wheat or barley in a large pot and cover it with plenty of water. Bring it to a boil, cover and reduce the heat for another ten minutes. Turn the heat off and leave the grains to cool and soak overnight. The next morning, the grains should have absorbed most of the liquid. Add the chickpeas, beans, rice, dried fruits, rosewater or orange and lemon zest and sugar.

Add more water to cover the ingredients only, if needed. Bring the mixture to a boil. Stir the mixture gently with a wooden spoon as it cooks until it thickens. Remove it from the heat and fill a large serving bowl or dessert bowls with the pudding. Once it cools down and sets, cover and refrigerate it for several hours. Before serving, garnish the pudding with fresh pomegranate seeds, pine nuts, finely chopped dried fruits and groundnuts.

Ice-cream and Watermelon Jelly

Preparation time: 12 minutes
Cooking Time: 70 minutes
Nutrition facts: 1 serving (212 Cal)

Ingredients (8 servings)

1 1/3 pounds of white sugar

4 oz of dessert wine

2 tablespoons of lemon

½ cup of orange juice

1 ½ pounds of strawberries

11 oz of watermelon, coarsely chopped

1 tablespoon of rosewater, or to taste

4 gelatin leaves, softened in cold water

3 cups of pouring cream

7 oz of milk

1/3 pound of strawberries, hulled and coarsely crushed

6 egg yolks

6 oz of caster sugar

1 ½ tablespoons of rosewater, or to taste

3 pieces of diced Turkish delight

Preparation

Set the jellies in individual serving bowls. In a large saucepan, mix the cream, milk and strawberries. Simmer over medium heat. Whisk the yolks, sugar and rosewater in a heatproof bowl until thick and pale; add the cream mixture and whisk again to combine. Return to the pan over medium heat, stirring continuously for 3-4 minutes or until the mixture coats the back of a wooden spoon thickly. Strain into a bowl over ice and refrigerate until chilled. Freeze in an ice-cream machine according to the manufacturer's instructions, then fold in Turkish delight and freeze until required.

Combine the sugar, wine, juices and 3 cups of water in a large saucepan, stir over medium-high heat until the sugar dissolves, then bring to a boil and cook for 2 minutes. Add the strawberries and watermelon, cook for 4-6 minutes or until pulpy. Remove from the heat and let it sit for 15 minutes. Process this with a hand-held blender, then transfer to a muslin-lined sieve placed over a large bowl and refrigerate for at least 6 hours.

Discard the solids. Add rosewater to the strawberry liquid, then transfer 8 oz of the juice to a small saucepan. Squeeze the excess water from gelatin, add to the pan and stir to dissolve over low heat. Return the gelatin mixture to the remaining strawberry liquid, pour into a 4 cup-capacity jelly mold and refrigerate overnight until set. Before serving, briefly dip the mold in hot water and pull the jelly away gently from the sides of the mold with your fingertips. Invert onto a serving plate and serve with Turkish delight ice-cream and some extra Turkish delight, if desired.

Baklava

Preparation time: 30 minutes
Cooking time: 100 minutes

Ingredients (24 servings)

22 sheets of dough

2 1/2 cups of cold water

3 1/2 cups of sugar

2 tablespoons of lemon juice

2 tablespoons of sugar

1 1/2 cups of unsalted clarified butter

2 packages of phyllo dough

Finely chopped pistachio nuts (optional)

3 cups of walnuts

Preparation

Heat the oven to 375 F. Combine the cold water with the sugar in a medium-sized saucepan. Boil the mixture for 5 minutes, then lower the heat and simmer, uncovered, for 14-16 minutes or until the syrup is light yellow and a small spoonful dropped onto a wooden surface and cooled is tacky. Stir the lemon juice into the syrup and set aside to cool.

Place the walnuts and sugar in a food processor. Process until medium to finely ground; do not grind too fine. Set aside.

Brush the inside of a 14 x 18 x 1-inch baking pan all over with a little of the clarified butter. Place 1 sheet of dough in the pan. With a wide pastry brush, lightly brush the dough with a little of the clarified butter. Continue layering the dough and brushing with butter until one package of dough is used completely. Spread the walnuts over the dough and lightly sprinkle it with water. Using a plant mister is best - to help the dough adhere to the walnuts when the next layer is added. Using the second package of the phyllo dough, layer the dough over the walnuts, brushing each sheet with a little bit of the butter. Trim the pastry edges to fit neatly in the baking pan. Brush the top layer and the edges with the clarified butter.

Using a sharp knife dipped in hot water, cut through the dough halfway down the height of the pan. To make 48 pieces, make 4 lengthwise cuts and 12 crosswise cuts. If you want to make triangle-shaped pastries, make 6 cuts crosswise instead of 12 and then cut diagonally across each rectangle. For diamond shapes, cut the dough diagonally in both directions.

Bake the baklava in the center of the oven for 28-32 minutes. Lower the heat to 325 F and bake for an additional 30 minutes, until the top is light golden. Remove from the oven and let it sit at room temperature for about 10 minutes. Recut the pastries along the lines all the way to the bottom of the baking pan and pour the cold syrup evenly over the cut lines. Sprinkle the baklava with ground walnuts or pistachio nuts if desired and let it cool completely before serving.

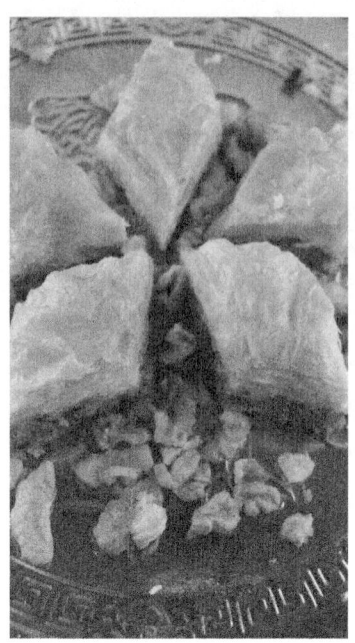

Saffron Pudding (*Zerde*)

Preparation: 40 minutes
Cooking time: 40 minutes

Ingredients (5 servings)

1/2 teaspoon of saffron

1 tablespoon of pine nuts

1 tablespoon of pomegranate seeds

1 tablespoon of pistachios, shelled and ground

1 tablespoon of currants

1/3 cup of short-grain rice

1 cup of sugar

1/3 cup of rosewater

3 tablespoons of arrowroot or cornstarch

Preparation

Soak the saffron in 1/4 cup of hot water for 22 minutes. At the same time, soak the currants in warm water for about 17 minutes. Drain them and set them aside. Meanwhile, place the rice and 4 1/2 cups of water in a medium-size saucepan and bring to a boil. Simmer the mixture for 27 minutes. Add the soaked saffron and its water along with the sugar, rosewater and arrowroot. Stir them well and simmer for about 5 minutes, until the pudding has thickened. Pour the pudding into individual serving cups and top with the pine nuts, currants, pomegranate seeds and pistachios. Cool the pudding for at least 40 minutes at room temperature before serving.

Feta Cheesecake (*Peynir Tatlisi*)

Preparation time: 130 minutes
Cooking time: 50 minutes

Ingredients (5 servings)
1 1/3 cups of good quality feta cheese
2 tablespoons of sugar
6 tablespoons of unsalted clarified butter
1 teaspoon of baking powder
3 tablespoons of heavy cream
3 room temperature eggs
1 cup of whole wheat flour, sifted
4 tablespoons of cornstarch

Syrup
3 cups of cold water
2 cups of sugar
1 tablespoon of lemon juice

Preparation
Cut the cheese into 1-inch cubes and soak them in a bowl of hot tap water for about 2 hours, changing the water frequently. Refrigerate the soaking cheese overnight so that all the salt leaches out. The next day, preheat the oven to 375 F and grease the bottom of a heavy-bottomed 14 x 18 x 1-inch baking pan with a little butter. Drain the cheese and squeeze out the excess water. Break it into small pieces by pushing it through a fine strainer into a bowl.

In another bowl, mix the sugar, butter and baking powder. Add the cheese and the cream and mix well with a wooden spoon. Add the eggs one at a time and blend them well. Add the flour and cornstarch and mix for about 1 minute, until all the ingredients are well incorporated. Do not overmix. Fill a 22 -inch piping bag, which has a large-tip star nozzle, with the mixture and pipe it onto the greased baking pan making 6 cakes, each 4 inches in diameter. Bake them for about 25 minutes, or until the tops are lightly colored.

In the meantime, make the syrup by combining the cold water with the sugar and bringing it to a boil. Boil it for 5 minutes, then lower the heat and simmer the syrup, uncovered, for about 15 minutes. Stir the lemon juice into the syrup and keep the syrup hot after you turn off the heat.

As soon as the cheesecakes are ready, pour 1/2 cup of warm water over them evenly and place another 1-inch-deep pan over them, upside down, making sure that it does not touch the cakes. Let the cakes rest for about 3 minutes.

Pour some of the hot syrup over the cakes, then lift each cake out, turn upside down and ladle the syrup over them. Keep turning the cakes a few more times in this manner, using up all the syrup. Cover the cakes and let them cool for at least 30 minutes at room temperature.

Turkish Rice Pudding (*Sutlac*)

Preparation time: 20 minutes
Cooking time: 40 minutes

Ingredients (5 servings)

1/2 cup of short-grain rice
4 1/4 cups of whole milk, divided
3 tablespoons of cornstarch
2 cups of water
1/4 cup of heavy cream
3/4 cup of sugar
Pinch of salt
1 tablespoon of vanilla extract
Ground cinnamon

Preparation

In a medium-sized saucepan, bring the rice in water to a boil over a high heat. Lower the heat, cover and cook very gently for 26-29 minutes or until the rice is tender and has absorbed the water. Stir in the 4 cups of milk, cream and sugar. Bring the mixture to a boil. Meanwhile, dissolve the cornstarch in the remaining 1/4 cup of the milk, then gradually add it to the boiling rice mixture, stirring constantly with a wooden spoon. Lower the heat to a medium, add a pinch of salt and the vanilla extract and simmer for about 14-17 minutes, uncovered. Stir frequently. Transfer the mixture to individual serving dishes and let it cool. Place in the refrigerator for several hours before serving.

PASTRIES

Pogaca

Preparation Time: 45 minutes
Cooking Time: 30 minutes
Nutrition facts: 1 serving (117 Cal)

Ingredients (12 servings)

2 egg yolks

1 tablespoon of water

5 cups of flour

7 oz of butter, softened

¾ cup of feta cheese, crumbled

2 tablespoons of parsley, chopped

1 cup of canola oil

1 cup of plain yogurt

2 teaspoons of baking powder

2 teaspoons of salt

2 teaspoons of nigella seeds for sprinkling

Preparation

Preheat the oven to 350 F. Combine feta and parsley in a bowl and set aside. In a small bowl, beat the egg yolks with a tablespoon of water. Set aside, since this will be used to brush the pogacas before baking. Place all the dough ingredients in a deep wide bowl. Mix thoroughly and knead with hands until the dough is elastic, non-sticky and smooth. Take a piece of the dough that is approximately the size of an egg and flatten on the palm of your hand. Place a teaspoon of filling in the center of the dough and close it up like a half-moon. Make sure the edges are pinched tightly, so that no filling can escape during the baking process. Place the pogacas on a piece of parchment paper on a cookie sheet (about 12 per sheet). Brush with the egg wash, sprinkle with nigella seeds and bake for 24-27 minutes or until golden brown.

Turkish Dumplings (*Manti*)

Preparation Time: 40 minutes
Cooking Time: 10 minutes
Nutrition facts: 1 dumpling (76 Cal)

Ingredients

Dough

1 cup of whole wheat flour

1 egg

1 teaspoon of salt

¼ cup of lukewarm water

Filling

7 oz of ground beef

1 onion, finely chopped

¼ bunch of parsley, finely chopped

½ teaspoon of salt

A pinch of black pepper

1 teaspoon of pepper paste

Yogurt Sauce and Butter Sauce

2 tablespoons of butter

1 tablespoon of olive oil

2 teaspoons of red pepper flakes or chili, sweet or hot

1 teaspoon of dried mint

4 cups of water to boil dumplings

1 cup of yogurt (for Yogurt sauce)

2 cloves of garlic, mashed (for Yogurt sauce)

A pinch of salt (for Yogurt sauce)

Preparation

Mix the flour, egg and salt. Add water gradually and mix with hand. Knead it well until your dough is a bit tough. Add the extra water or flour to have this result. Make a ball from it and roll it out not so thin, about ¾ inch thick. Cut it into strips first, then into small squares. Place a little filling on each square. Close them up patiently. Heat 4 cups of water in a pot and add the dumplings when it boils. Boil them for about 9-11 minutes or until softened. Transfer them into plates with a slotted spoon. Mix all the ingredients of yogurt sauce. Melt the butter and add in the olive oil. Add the dried mint and red pepper flakes in, stir. Use it after about 20 seconds. Pour some yogurt on dumplings and drizzle a little oil sauce over them before serving.

Catal

Preparation Time: 20 minutes
Cooking Time: 20 minutes
Nutrition facts: 1 serving (165 Cal)

Ingredients (15 servings)

4 oz of soft margarine or butter

½ cup of low-fat yogurt

½ cup of whole yogurt

3 oz of olive oil

1 egg

1 tablespoon of sesame seeds/nigella seeds

1 pound of flour

1 tablespoon of sugar

¼ teaspoon of salt

2 tablespoons of vinegar

1 tablespoon of baking powder

Preparation

In a bowl, mix the yogurt, egg, margarine, vinegar and baking powder. Gradually add flour and mix until you get a non-sticky soft dough. Place the dough on a plain surface, divide into walnut-sized balls and roll each to a rope using hands. Now fold the cord to create a wide "S" shape, so that the width is about twice the height. Now pinch the sides of the S to develop an oval shape with three strands and lay them in a greased pan or a baking sheet. Mix an egg yolk with a teaspoon of oil and brush the pastries. Sprinkle the sesame seeds. Bake at 350 F for 18-22 minutes or until golden brown.

Turkish Spinach Pastry

Preparation Time: 15 minutes
Cooking Time: 10 minutes
Nutrition facts: 1 pastry (106 Cal)

Ingredients (6 servings)
Dough
3 cups of flour
1 pack of dry yeast
¼ teaspoon of salt

Filling
1 pound of spinach
2 chopped onions
4 oz of white or feta cheese

Preparation
In a mixing bowl, add the flour, yeast and salt and mix well until a soft and smooth dough is formed. Cover it with a plastic foil and leave it to rise. In the meantime, fry the onions until golden. Add the spinach, cook until soft and let it cool down. Crumble feta cheese with hands and add to the cooked spinach. When the dough is ready, make balls about the size of a golf ball and flatten them to a disc using a dough roller.

Put a teaspoon full of the spinach filling on one side of the disc and fold the empty side over to create a half-circle. Pinch the edges of the half-circle to seal the dough around the stuffing. Bake in the oven at 375 F until golden. Remove from the oven and brush the surface with olive oil.

Turkish Spinach Pie

Preparation Time: 15 minutes
Cooking Time: 40 minutes
Nutrition facts: 1 serving (429 Cal)

Ingredients (12 servings)
20 Phyllo sheets

Spinach Filling
3 packages of frozen spinach, defrosted and drained of water
¼ cup of feta cheese, crumbled
1 egg
A small bunch of fresh parsley, roughly chopped
A small bunch of fresh mint, roughly chopped
Salt and pepper to taste

Glaze
1/3 cup of milk
¼ cup of olive oil
6 tablespoons of butter, melted and solids removed
1 egg
1/3 cup of milk and 1 egg for toping

Preparation
Unfold the phyllo and place on a dry clean surface. Have a lightly damp towel close to cover as you're layering. In a large bowl, mix all the spinach filling ingredients well. In a separate bowl, mix the glaze and a third bowl, mix the topping glaze.

Brush a 9 x 13 pan on all sides and the bottom with the glaze mixture. Layer the first layer of pastry into the pan and brush with the glaze. Continue this for ten layers. Add the spinach filling and distribute it evenly. Then top with phyllo and continue to add layers, apply the glaze in between the layers with the help of a brush. When all the phyllo sheets are layered, the top layer should be brushed again with the glazing mixture. With the help of a sharp knife, cut the layered sheets into 12 squares or 24 triangles. Bake at 350 F for 38-42 minutes or until the top begins to brown.

Yumurtali Pide

Preparation Time: 12 minutes
Cooking time: 10 minutes
Nutrition facts: 1 serving (193 Cal)

Ingredients (8 servings)

Topping

2 oz of medium cheddar cheese, thinly sliced

4 oz of grated mozzarella

½ of a medium tomato, deseeded and thinly sliced

¼ of a green bell pepper, cut in half and thinly sliced

2 eggs (one egg for each pide, over topping)

Red pepper flakes

Dough

11 oz of all-purpose plain flour

2 teaspoons of dried yeast

1 teaspoon of sugar

1 teaspoon of salt

1/2 cup of warm water

⅓ cup of warm milk

3 tablespoons of olive oil

1 teaspoon of olive oil to brush the pide

Preparation

Preheat the oven to 350 F. Stir the dried yeast and sugar in a small bowl and pour in ½ cup of warm water. Dissolve and mix the yeast in water. Set aside for 4-6 minutes, for the yeast mixture to get frothy. Combine the flour and salt in a large bowl. Make a well in the middle and pour 2 tablespoons of olive oil and the yeast mixture in. Stir the warm milk into the flour mixture. Using hands, draw the flour in from the sides and work the mixture into a dough. Knead on a floured surface for 3-5 minutes, until you reach a soft, smooth dough. The dough may get sticky as you knead, so pour the remaining 1 tablespoon of olive oil in and add a little more flour if needed, to help shape into a soft dough. Grease a large bowl with a little olive oil, place the dough on it and cover with a cling film. Leave the dough in a warm place for 70 minutes to rise.

Once the dough rises, place it on a lightly floured surface. Knead the dough for a minute, then divide it into two pieces and roll into two balls. On a lightly floured surface, roll the dough balls into 2 oval shapes of 8 inch x 16 inch, with 1/5 inch thickness. Line a large baking tray with a baking paper and place the 2 flat bread dough ovals on the tray.

Spread the grated mozzarella cheese, cheddar cheese, sliced peppers and tomatoes evenly over the 2 flat pieces of bread, leaving 1 inch on the edges without filling as a border. Fold in the sides to act as a border to keep the filling intact. Squeeze the oval dough on each end to make it pointy. Beat an egg in a small bowl and mix it with 1 teaspoon of olive oil. Brush the edges of the dough with this mixture. Bake for 18-20 minutes or until the sides are golden and crispy at the edges. Take the pide tray out of the oven and carefully crack an egg in the middle of each pide. Return to the oven and bake for another 4-5 minutes. Do not overcook; the yolk should still be runny.

If you liked Turkish food, discover to how cook *DELICIOUS* recipes from other Balkan countries!

Within these pages, you'll learn 35 authentic recipes from a Balkan cook. These aren't ordinary recipes you'd find on the Internet, but recipes that were closely guarded by our Balkan mothers and passed down from generation to generation.

Main Dishes, Appetizers, and Desserts included!

If you want to learn how to make Croatian green peas stew, and 32 other authentic Balkan recipes, then start with our book!

Order on Amazon now for only $2,99!

If you're a Mediterranean dieter who wants to know the secrets of the Mediterranean diet, dieting, and cooking, then you're about to discover how to master cooking meals on a Mediterranean diet right now!

In fact, if you want to know how to make Mediterranean food, then this new e-book - "The 30-minute Mediterranean diet" - gives you the answers to many important questions and challenges every Mediterranean dieter faces, including:

How can I succeed with a Mediterranean diet?

What kind of recipes can I make?

What are the key principles to this type of diet?

What are the suggested weekly menus for this diet?

Are there any cheat items I can make?

... and more!

If you're serious about cooking meals on a Mediterranean diet and you really want to know how to make Mediterranean food, then you need to grab a copy of "The 30-minute Mediterranean diet" right now.

Prepare **111 recipes with several ingredients in less than 30 minutes!**

Order on Amazon now for only $2,99!

What could be better than a home-cooked meal? Maybe only a Greek homemade meal.

Do not get discouraged if you have no Greek roots or friends.

Now you can make a Greek food feast in your kitchen.

This ultimate Greek cookbook offers you 111 best dishes of this cuisine! From more famous gyros to more exotic *Kota Kapama* this cookbook keeps it easy and affordable.

All the ingredients necessary are wholesome and widely accessible.

The author's picks are as flavorful as they are healthy. The dishes described in this cookbook are "what Greek mothers have made for decades."

Full of well-balanced and nutritious meals, this handy cookbook includes many vegan options.
Discover a plethora of benefits of Mediterranean cuisine, and you may fall in love with cooking at home.

Inspired by a real food lover, this collection of delicious recipes will taste buds utterly satisfied.

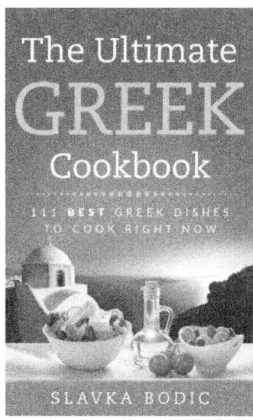

Order on Amazon now for only $2,99!

Maybe to try exotic Serbian cuisine?

From succulent *sarma*, soups, warm and cold salads to delectable desserts, the plethora of flavors will satisfy the most jaded foodie. Have a taste of a new culture with this **traditional Serbian cookbook**.

Order on Amazon now for only $2,99!

ONE LAST THING

If you enjoyed this book or found it useful I'd be very grateful if you could find the time to post a short review on Amazon. Your support really does make a difference and I read all the reviews personally, so I can get your feedback and make this book even better.

Thanks again for your support!

Please send me your feedback at
www.balkanfood.org

Printed in Great Britain
by Amazon

43494197R00116